RONALD GREGOR SMITH

J. G. HAMANN

1730–1788

A Study in Christian Existence

WITH SELECTIONS FROM
HIS WRITINGS

COLLINS
ST JAMES'S PLACE, LONDON
1960

In Memoriam

TAGE SCHACK

A writer who is in haste to be understood to-day and to-morrow runs the danger of being forgotten the day after to-morrow.

HAMANN *to* F. H. JACOBI
10 *March*, 1788

CONTENTS

PREFACE

THE HAMANN specialist will know of the difficulty of securing even some of the standard source books. The bibliography attached to the present study contains several which I was able only to consult at various times from University libraries in Britain and Germany. A very thorough, and indeed model, bibliography of Hamanniana is now available in the first volume of the new commentaries, *Hamanns Hauptschriften erklärt*. When measured against this bibliography, with its accompanying detailed historical study of Hamann interpretation, the present work is no more than an essay in modern interpretation, and a signpost to the extraordinary rich field which still awaits cultivation. For instance, the relations of Hamann to the British empiricists, the truth and the defect in his view of Kant, his relation to Luther, his views on education (with their influence on Nicolovius, then on Wilhelm von Humboldt, and through him on the Prussian educational system), are all clearly topics of the greatest interest, which are here only indicated.

But even with the actual texts to hand—both in Nadler's definitive edition of the works and in the old and precious Roth edition (still in spite of *lacunæ* and some arbitrariness in the editing the more congenial edition to handle)—the difficulty of making adequate translations can be appreciated only by those who have tried their hand at translating Hamann—unfortunately for me, only a few people. My friend, Mr. Stanley Godman, kindly let me consult translations he had made of selections from the *Biblical Reflections* and of the *Fragments*, and I have been helped by seeing the quotations—only too few—translated by

Canon Walter Lowrie and Professor J. C. O'Flaherty in their respective studies.

It is common for translators to lament their difficulties, thus indirectly praising their achievement and at the same time trying to soften the hard critic. But on this occasion I am able to summon Goethe to my aid. He wrote of being " fatigued and led astray by so many riddles " in Hamann's language; he remarked that in reading *Golgatha und Scheblimini* it was not always possible to follow the author the first time; and concluded his account (in a letter to Charlotte von Stein, 17 September, 1784) with the words: " on peut bien affirmer la paradox qu'on ne l'entend pas par l'entendement."

In the task of going through the texts, and helping to select as well as translate, my wife has been tremendously patient and helpful.

The whole task has been greatly eased by the notable labours of Professor Josef Nadler, who in addition to providing a most comprehensive biography and a completely documented edition of the *Werke* has recently (1957) published an additional sixth volume, which is nothing less than a highly compressed commentary, concordance and dictionary of all the difficult allusions to persons and literature which fill Hamann's writings. Once the more elaborate Schreiner-Blanke commentaries on the chief texts are complete, Hamann will have emerged as much as possible from obscurity.

The most instructive and rounded study of Hamann's life and thought might well have been that of the Danish scholar Tage Schack. Only twelve out of the planned twenty-one chapters were completed before his tragic death, in April, 1945, in the service of the truth, during the German occupation of Denmark. As it is, the published chapters provide an illuminating study of Hamann in our time and for our time. This work is unfortunately not available in English, and in dedicating my study to his memory I wish to indicate my debt to him. My only serious point of difference with him concerns the measure in which he interprets Hamann in terms of Kierkegaard.

For Hamann cannot be subjected to wholesale systematisation. He will always be enigmatic, and illuminating in snatches, like lightning flashing across a rich and mysterious landscape. It is this consideration which has persuaded me—along with more humdrum considerations of the space and size that can be expected of an English introduction—to give nothing more than an extended anthology of his writings in English. The task of putting the whole of Hamann into English is virtually impossible; but even if it were done, it is doubtful whether it would be productive. But perhaps others with other interests, especially literary and philosophical, will now be encouraged to delve into the material which awaits them.

Lastly, it is my pleasant duty to thank the Maurice Trustees who invited me to deliver the F. D. Maurice Lectures for 1958 at King's College, London. The present study is an enlarged version of those lectures. I have happy recollections of the kindness and hospitality of the Senate of King's College, especially of the Dean, the Rev. Sidney Evans.

University of Glasgow,   R. G. S.
August, 1958

Christian Existence

I

INTRODUCTORY

JOHANN GEORG HAMANN is not well known in the English-speaking world. There is no full study of his life and work in English. A pamphlet by the American Kierkegaard scholar, the late Walter Lowrie, published in 1950,[1] and a study of Hamann's views on language by the American scholar, Professor J. C. O'Flaherty,[2] are the only independent productions known to me. These, with a handful of articles in learned journals, constitute the total of Hamanniana in English. In other languages there is a certain trickle of interest, while in German the interest has been more intimate and more complicated. Since the time of Goethe's respectful but somewhat desultory and distant acknowledgment of Hamann's greatness, and Hegel's brilliant review of the first edition of Hamann's works,[3] German interest in Hamann, though often one-sided, has never quite died down. In our own time, with the publication for the first time of the complete works,[4] and the work in progress both on a complete edition of the letters,[5] and on a series of commentaries on the main texts,[6] it is even possible to speak of a small renaissance of Hamann.

[1] *Hamann—an Existentialist*, Princeton, 1950.
[2] *Unity and Language*, Chapel Hill, 1952.
[3] See *Sämtliche Werke*, ed. Glockner, vol. 20, 1930.
[4] Ed. J. Nadler, Vienna, in five volumes, 1949-53. A sixth volume, 1957, consists of an index which is at the same time a splendid dictionary of Hamann's ideas and allusions. (Hereafter quoted as NI, etc.)
[5] *Johann Georg Hamann Briefwechsel*, edited by W. Ziesemer and A. Henkel, in eight volumes, of which volumes I-III have so far appeared, Wiesbaden 1955, 1956, 1957. (Hereafter quoted as BI, etc.)
[6] *J. G. Hamanns Hauptschriften erklärt*, ed. F. Blanke and L. Schreiner, to appear in eight volumes, of which I and VII have been published, Gütersloh, 1956.

The present essay, and the translation of parts of the writings and letters, are intended as a provisional remedy for the English-speaking world. My particular theological interests are bound to be reflected in my treatment; but I hope I have avoided too tendentious an approach. Certainly, Hamann's interests were not narrow. He has been called "the first Christian *Literat*" or man of letters,[1] and whatever the description is intended to include, at least it excludes any idea of a professional system-builder.

Hamann is of course known to students of German literature as the enigmatic figure in the background of the *Sturm und Drang*, that movement of the spirit and of letters which preceded, and precipitated, the Romantic movement in German life and literature. He is also known to students of philosophy as a marginal figure in the life of Immanuel Kant, whose contemporary and fellow-citizen and friend he was in Königsberg. In more recent theological writing he has become the object of a certain amount of interest as one of the few writers who had a marked influence on Kierkegaard. In fact it would, I believe, be possible to detect in the writings of Hamann, in embryonic or sibylline form at least, almost all the major concerns of Kierkegaard. The connections between the two will be apparent to any student of Kierkegaard. Perhaps if the connection had been closer, Kierkegaard would have stood more in the centre of theological interests than he does.

This is not the place to say much about Kierkegaard. But since the interest of many readers of Hamann may well take its rise, as my own has done, in the study of Kierkegaard,[2] perhaps a preliminary judgment is not out of place. A typical appraisal of the relative positions of the two men is that of Karlfried Gründer,

---

[1] E. Hirsch, *Geschichte der neueren evangelischen Theologie*, Gütersloh, 1952, IV, 177.

[2] While Kierkegaard led me formally back to Hamann, I should not omit mention of Ferdinand Ebner, *Das Wort und die Geistigen Realitäten*, Regensburg, 1921. This work, though fragmentary and undeveloped, connects Hamann's view of the Word with a kind of Christian personalism. His book still awaits a translator.

in the first volume of the splendidly planned commentaries on Hamann's main works. He writes:

> That God in incomprehensible reconciling grace lowers himself (has entered into human life, *Dasein*, as Kierkegaard says) is central alike for Kierkegaard and for Hamann. For Hamann it is also, and precisely, the world which God enters, but for Kierkegaard the place of this event is solely the individual, who in the decision of his faith, effected by grace, rises above the world, with which the " humorist " [in this case Hamann] continues to identify the " idea of God."[1]

Kierkegaard, in other words, reaches a point beyond the world, the point of religious passion, in which the individual faces God, God alone, in the decision of inwardness, of pure subjectivity. That is why it is possible for Kierkegaard to say that there is even a certain " blasphemy " in Hamann's words, that " he would rather hear the truth from a Pharisee against his will than from an angel of light."[2] For Kierkegaard there is another stage, the stage of directness, of the " single one " separated from the world, which is beyond humour. For Hamann there is no stage beyond the indirectness of faith, which is grounded in the whole life of the world and history. God is certainly transcendent, for Hamann as for Kierkegaard; but Hamann hears and responds to the Word as a Word in the present, which means in the whole present connection of life in this world. Hamann therefore understands the relation to God not as something in and for itself, separate from the world, but in and through the world. He remains a " humorist "; there is for him no religious stage beyond that of humour. That is to say, his faith includes, and never gives up, scepticism. He combines believing and not believing within the conditions of this world.

[1] *Hamanns Hauptschriften erklärt*, I, 50.
[2] Kierkegaard, *Papirer*, II, A, 12; Hamann, letter to Lindner, 12 October, 1759, R I, 497 = B I, 431.

It is this less absolute position, then, which distinguishes Hamann from his admirer Kierkegaard. Kierkegaard lamented that Michelet had reduced Hamann to a paragraph. " The system is hospitable,"[1] and could even classify and dispose of Hamann's protest against a system of life. But Kierkegaard himself did something similar to Hamann. For the intimate connections between the two should not obscure the fact that in the end Kierkegaard found Hamann too much bound to the world and not enough to God. But in the last analysis Kierkegaard himself, desiring to be alone in the world with God, that is, without the world, was also in a real sense without God. It is the wholeness of God's condescension in Christ, his complete entering into the world through his Word, which engaged Hamann's life; but Kierkegaard, the great preacher of the " offence " of Christianity, could not in the end live with it. He wanted " directness." Hamann, content with receiving what was given in and through the world, has scarcely had a hearing. It is as though the immense implications of his tumultuous insights were too much, not only for himself, but also for his readers.

The conviction which guides the present study is that in Hamann we have a man who saw and who felt in his own life the unsolved problem of the modern world—how to be a Christian in full integrity of being: by which I mean something more than, yet including, intellectual integrity. That Hamann did in a measure solve that problem for his own life, in terms of a positive understanding of the Word in history and for faith, is the view implicit in the interpretation given here.

In the realm of Christian orthodoxy to-day there is a tendency to claim that this problem has been solved along other lines. In particular, what Paul Tillich calls " kerygmatic theology "[2] proposes an authoritarian proclamation, claiming the assent of

---

[1] *Concluding Unscientific Postscript*, E.T., 224.
[2] *Systematic Theology*, Chicago, 1951, I, 4ff.

faith, which leads to a life of thorough obedience to a specific world-view. On the other hand there is a claim from the side of what is almost a new, para-Christian, orthodoxy, which passes under various names—scientism, naturalism, materialism, humanism—but which in general reflects a mood of agnosticism tinged with mild, or furious, despair. Here the problem is reduced by excision of the Christian element, and integrity consists in recognising man's destiny without admitting God or revelation. The two claims are diametrically opposed. They unite only in opposing the claim of a man like Hamann to have anything significant to say. For the "kerygmatic" theologian Hamann is too self-willed, too much of a poet and an individual, too much of an existentialist (in a sense which I hope to make clear), too little of a dogmatist. For the modern literary critic and "humanist" he is simply ineffective. Thus Professor Roy Pascal writes of him that his religion "transparently betrays his unwillingness or incapacity to face up to the tasks of active and practical life."[1] It is necessary to say categorically, in opposition to this judgment, that all the evidence shows us that Hamann was in truth neither unable nor unwilling to face the tasks of life. More, it is even possible to see both in his thought and in his life the adumbration of a way which surpasses the difference between the dogmatist and the humanist, the common and still unsolved modern conflict between "faith" and "reason," or orthodoxy and unbelief, or "reaction" and "progress." The revolution which the *Aufklärung* brought to Europe, and in particular to the ways of thought and life within the Christian tradition of Europe, was faced by Hamann in full consciousness of its immense import. His effort to point towards an integrated life of faith is worthy of our attention, in a time when there seems to be so little understanding between the opposing camps which clamour for human loyalty.

[1] *The German Sturm and Drang*, London, 1951, 93.

21

The method of the present study of the " Magus in the north," however, as he was called, and liked to call himself,[1] needs a little more explanation. His published works are incapable of systematic treatment. His style may not unjustly be described as tumultuous, obscure and perverse. Even his many extant letters, which are written for the most part without the labour and forethought so apparent in the works, and which are often delightful specimens of sheer unforced humour, humanity and vivacity, are nevertheless always highly allusive, often fugitive, and throughout intensely personal. No doubt it is a challenge for his readers to try to penetrate what Hegel called the " concentrated intensity " of Hamann's " spiritual depth," " without any expansion either of the imagination or of thought."[2] But no student of Hamann would, I think, contest the conclusion that no writing of his is completely transparent. His only thoroughly legible composition—though it too is not entirely transparent— is his own life. And his writings must be read as a reflection of this life, or as a witness to it.[3]

But the chaos which his writings present even to patient study is not entirely involuntary. Admittedly, some part of the disorder is involuntary. Here we may take Hamann's words at most of their face value, when, for instance, he writes:

I have no aptitude for truths, principles, systems; but for crumbs, fragments, fancies, sudden inspirations.[4]

---

[1] It was Friedrich Karl von Moser who first used the words, in direct allusion to Hamann's seeing the Star of Bethlehem, like the wise men from the east, in a time without Christ. Cf. F. Blanke, *Hamann-Studien*, Zürich, 1956, 99. The earliest reference is in a letter of 1760: "You have seen the star; let others run after the will-o'-the-wisp " (quoted in J. Disselhoff, *Wegweiser zu J. G. Hamann*, Kaiserswerth 1871, 3).

[2] In his long review of the edition of the *Schriften* by F. Roth, 1828 (*Sämtliche Werke*, Jubiläumsausgabe, Stuttgart, 1930, XX, 240ff.).

[3] Cf. " My authorship is in such exact connexion with my outward circumstances that each is a part of the whole." (Letter to F. H. Jacobi, 7 December, 1786, G 444—i.e., Vol. V of C. H. Gildemeister, *J. G. Hamann's, des Magus im Norden, Leben und Schriften*, Gotha, 1868.)

[4] Letter to J. G. Lindner, 12 October, 1759, B I, 431.

But over and above this I believe it is possible to discern in the course of his life, his choices, his responsibilities, his renunciations and even what seemed to the good sense of his time his irresponsibilities, a form and order which are not, it is true, to be judged by æsthetic or prudential maxims; which owe nothing to the contemporary view of healthy human reason or harmonious good sense; which are, in fact, the form and order of a truly Christian existence. And it is this existence, which is irreducible to maxims or a system, to which his unsystematic writings continually point. "System is in itself a hindrance to the truth," he wrote on another occasion to Jacobi,[1] and here too we must take him at his word. It is precisely the conjunction of his personal dislike of system with his love for the fragmentary and the sudden inspiration which leads him to see the truth in Christian existence as going beyond the formal and objective statement of it. It is not that he defiantly flaunts his own weakness in regard to system and clarity, and his own partiality for brief, pregnant, allusive and obscure remarks; but rather that he perceives in his very weakness the only way for any human being to try to face the enigma of his own existence.

But obviously for any expositor of his thought a real problem is here brought to the fore. The only possible method is to try to point through the works and the thought to the life. The life is everything—even though it too is fragmentary and incomplete, a pointer to possibilities rather than their empirical fulfilment or fruition. Yet a strict biography in the whole context of the time is beyond the scope and competence of the present study. This matters the less as chronological succession plays little or no part in Hamann's thought. Development, in fact, is alien to his whole way of life. His life may rather be seen as an existential composition, full of contradictions, with nothing smooth, and nothing hidden, in which recurrent convictions illuminate in

[1] G 228.

turn the outward events, and the many friends and enemies with whom he was actively engaged all his life. For this composition is not formed along the lines of the *cogito ergo sum* of the rationalist world in which he lived, but of the *Est ergo cogito* of a Christian existentialist.[1] It is, at any rate, only in these terms that it has seemed possible to try to comprehend, and to present, his many-sided interests, as literary critic, essayist, translator, reviewer, philologist, æsthetician, philosopher and theologian, as having at least the outline of a single whole.

[1] Letter of 2 June, 1785, to Jacobi, G 81; cf. G 196: " Do not forget the noble *sum* on account of the *cogito;*" and G 476: " In the kitchen, too, the gods are to be found; and what Descartes says about his *cogito* is brought home to me by the activity of my stomach."

2

OUTLINE
OF HAMANN'S LIFE

IT IS fundamental to an understanding of Hamann to see his thought and his actions as thoroughly integrated. The thought cannot be separated from the life, and though the life is everything, it is so as an expression of the thought. Neither his life nor his thought is an object which can be systematised, classified, and held up for public admiration or censure. The very nature of the integration of the life and the thought is that it precludes any such objectifying. For all his love of mysteries and pseudonyms as an author, Hamann is fundamentally an open, indeed a lovable, person. He does not make any distinction between his private and his public life. He is not different as an author from what he is in his ordinary life. In Philip Merlan's acute words,

> Hamann would have been ashamed had there been any difference between his private and his public communications... He never addressed the public. He spoke as if to his personal acquaintances and he spoke strictly as a private person. Long before Kierkegaard he wrote in the style of " the single one " and wrote for " the single one." In this sense of the word, he never tried to be " objective."[1]

With this basic proviso, then, that to " objectify " the events of Hamann's life does not correspond to the basic unity of person in his authorship and his actions, a bare outline of Hamann's life will nevertheless help to ease the reader's way. The present outline will so far as possible avoid problems and explanations: it

[1] *Claremont Quarterly*, April, 1955, 35.

is intended simply as a help in orientation. But the reader's complaisance must be requested, for a skeleton of this kind continually demands to be clothed with flesh and blood. It is therefore impossible to avoid a certain amount of repetition in the whole account. If you try to talk about Hamann's life by itself, his ideas come crowding in, and when you talk about his ideas they begin to make sense only by reference to the events of his life. For the events, in essence, flow from the decisions of his faith.

Johann Georg Hamann was born in Königsberg on 27 August, 1730. He was the grandson of a Lutheran pastor, and the elder son of a surgeon—chirurgeon might indicate better the old-fashioned style of his art—who as *Alststadtbader* was also in charge of the public bathing establishment of the old town. He was a respected citizen, who refused the honourable title of *Hof Rat*. In his home many of the well-known citizens of Könisberg might be met. An uncle of our Hamann, bearing the same name, published religious verses, some of which were set to music by Telemann and Handel.

In 1730 Kant was six years old, Lessing and Moses Mendelssohn about a year old. It was still fourteen years till Herder's birth, nineteen till Goethe's.

The small family, with two sons, lived comfortably. The afternoon coffee-hour, established even then as the mark of German bourgeois respectability, was regularly honoured by the household. In the town itself, busy and prosperous, many languages could be heard: Dutch, English, Polish, Russian, the Scandinavian and Baltic languages, as well as German. Hamann's ear must have been early attuned to hearing distinctions of language. Königsberg was a microcosm of the busy, flourishing, progressive world of eighteenth century Europe.

After some time at private schools, and then at the Kneiphof school, Johann Georg matriculated at the university at the age of sixteen. The outstanding teacher was Martin Knutzen, professor of philosophy and mathematics, who was also Kant's teacher. Hamann always spoke of him with great respect. Knutzen united pietist beliefs with Wolffian rationalist methods of thought. But one of his remarks—that " the penitent spends in grief and weeping the time which he ought to be using for doing good "—indicates how far his pietism had developed a rationalist cast. The professor of physics, Karl Heinrich Rappolt, to whom Hamann felt more personally attracted, probably on account of the combination of humour and humanism in his character, was a pronounced enemy of pietism. It is probable, however, that no marked outside influence on the young student may be singled out. His studies were desultory and self-willed, and though he officially switched early from theology to law, his main interests ranged through the *belles lettres* of modern Europe. His lifelong passion, for wide and intense reading—to which indeed his earlier schooling had also inclined him—was already apparent.

At the university he made his first real friends, chief among them Johann Gotthelf Lindner (1729-1776) and Johann Christoph Berens (1729-1782). Lindner became rector of the cathedral school in Riga, and in 1765 professor of poetry at Königsberg, ending as Lutheran minister of Löbenicht/Königsberg. He was Hamann's confidant throughout his life, though at times he found it hard to avoid scolding Hamann, and Hamann for his part sometimes found his friend lacking in understanding. With Berens and the large family of this Riga merchant house Hamann's relations were intense and decisive for his career. With these two and others Hamann founded in 1749 a weekly periodical, *Daphne*, which lasted for sixty issues. This was not exactly an original venture, but it showed the alertness of the young Königsberg student group of friends to the great world of letters. Nadler, Hamann's modern biographer, calls *Daphne*

27

" one of the best weeklies of the century," but this is an audacious judgment in face of the *Spectator*, the *Tatler* and the *Rambler*.

In November 1752 Hamann left the university without taking a degree, and became house-tutor in a Baltic noble family of Kegeln, near Papendorf. The boy whom he had to educate was not an easy first pupil for the inexperienced teacher. But Hamann at once showed a power to teach which is as marked as his failure to impress the ordinary successful people of his time. The baroness, the boy's mother, dismissed the too conscientious teacher inside six months, in a letter which is a fearsome example of stupidity, illiteracy and arrogance, which unfortunately defies translation. Hamann's second post, at Grünhof near Mitau, was happier. Here was an ordered, polished and lively society. With one break, spent in Riga, Hamann stayed in this household till 1756. Then the much-travelled and fascinating friend, J. C. Berens, back in Riga from Göttingen and Paris, persuaded him to take a post in his family business. Hamann with his knowledge of languages and extensive experience must have seemed a potentially most useful acquisition. Before he had left Grünhof he had made a translation of Dangeuil's *Remarques sur les avantages et les désavantages de la France et de la Grande Bretagne par rapport au commerce et aux autres sources de la puissance des États*, which was published, along with a supplement by himself, in April 1756. (This supplement was actually published in an English translation, the only translation made of any work of Hamann's before the present volume, in New York, under the title *The Merchant*, 4th edition 1856.) This publication sets the tone in which Hamann accepted work with the house of Berens. His supplement is in effect praise of the new society which under the leadership of the new race, the merchants, was to serve man as part of the divine plan. Hamann was ready to become a useful and serviceable member of this society. He was never to be in closer accord with the world of the Enlightenment than he was at this time.

The fateful events of the next two years are recounted in his autobiography. In April 1757 he went to London as an emissary of the Berens family, on an obscure mission which apparently involved negotiations with the Russian and English governments concerning trade in the Baltic. But the English were too occupied with their American colonies to spare time for the East, and the mission failed. Hamann returned to Riga in July 1758, a changed man. In the eyes of the Berens family the change was a disaster. Hamann to them was denying the age of reason and his own past. For he had become what they could only regard as a bigoted Christian. Christoph Berens skimmed the pages of Hamann's London *Thoughts about my Life* " with loathing."[1] It was on this point that the real difference arose. Hamann's engagement to Katharina Berens came to nothing. It is true that, like Kierkegaard later, his broken-off engagement continued to influence him, and probable that this influence played some part in the strange circumstances of his marriage. He regarded Katharina Berens as his " bride from God's hand." Nevertheless, the decisive break lay deep in Hamann's self-understanding.

His friends did not let him go without a struggle. Berens followed him to Königsberg in June 1759, full of a clever plan to entice Hamann back to reason. In Königsberg that summer there followed an episode which Hamann has described in his letters, particularly to Kant. For it was none other than the Privatdozent for *Himmelsmechanik* or astronomy and physics who was chosen by Berens to meet Hamann and do his best to restore him to his senses. Hamann found the situation ludicrous, and for Kant it was tiresome. This is the first clear point in the relations between Kant and Hamann, the significance of which will be discussed in more detail later. Kant tried to persuade Hamann to translate some articles from the French *Encyclopédie*, to encourage him in a career as a writer, and so to wean him from the

[1] Cf. letter to J. G. Lindner, 21 March, 1759, B I, 308.

life of bigoted orthodoxy into which he imagined Hamann had relapsed. But it was precisely in virtue of his new self-understanding that Hamann refused to conform. He would go his own way, which he understood in terms of Socrates's life, who was not an author—and in explaining himself, in the *Socratic Memorabilia* (1759), he became, in his own peculiar way, an author by contradiction. (All his writing was to be of this kind —personal, occasional, and published only as the reflection of an occasion and of the personal standpoint of the author within the occasion.) The book was a manifesto of a way of life, and bore a double dedication, to " Nobody " (the public) and to " the two " (Kant and Berens). Hamann was convinced of the rightness of his decision, even against this powerful combination of the philosopher and the man of affairs, who together, as Nadler has said, represented " the whole kingdom of total reason."[1]

Twenty-five years later, Hamann was reading the proofs of the *Critique of Pure Reason* even before its author, and shaping the criticisms which he finally published as the *Metacritique of the Purism of Reason*. Both then, in 1784, towards the end of his life, and in this first encounter of 1759, when his future was still unclear, Hamann's criticism of Kant was fundamentally the same:

Once for all, my Herr Magister, I want to remove the hope from you that you can discuss certain things with me, which I can judge better than you, for I know more data about them, and base myself on *facta*, and do not know *my* authors from journals [*scil.* of the *Aufklärung*], but from laborious daily pondering; and have read, not extracts, but the very acts in which the King's interest as well as the land's are debated [*scil.* the Scriptures] . . .[2]

[1] *Johann Georg Hamann*, Vienna, 1949, 110.   [2] Letter of 27 July, 1759, B I, 379.

Again, in the middle years, in a correspondence in 1774 concerning Herder, Hamann was still saying much the same thing to Kant. He writes:

> While truth in general is of such an abstract and intellectual nature that it cannot be grasped except *in abstracto*, which is its element, [yet] *in concreto* truth appears either as a contradiction or as that stone of our wise men, by means of which every unripe mineral, and even stone and wood, are changed into pure gold.[1]

It was in the concrete and contradictory realm of human actions and human personality that Hamann tried to communicate with Kant. Kant saw no future in action like Hamann's, which he regarded as fettered to dogmas; and he spoke with assurance of the development of the work of men like the orientalist Michaelis of Göttingen and of " free-believing philologians," from whom the " demagogues " (the theologians) would in future have to take the material for the instruction of their students. " For there stands against him [Herder, the author of the *Älteste Urkunde des Menschengeschlechts*] the solid phalanx of the masters of Oriental learning."[2] But Hamann was always clear that " the foundation of our faith " did not rest " in the quicksand of fashionable critical scholarship."[3] In our own time, under the influence of Kierkegaard's thought in particular, the issue of the relation of Christian faith to history is very lively, and at least it can be said that Kant's view has by no means prevailed—even though the position represented by Hamann does not dominate either.

Once the break, then, with his past was clear, the succeeding years, from 1759 till 1763, unfolded in accordance with Hamann's

---

[1] Letter of April, 1774, B III, 88.
[2] Quoted in H. Weber, *Hamann und Kant*, Munich, 1904, 146.
[3] *Christiani Zacchaei Telonarchae Prolegomena über die neueste Auslegung der ältesten Urkunde des menschlichen Geschlechts*, 1774, R IV, 198 = N III, 132.

own decision. Characteristically, he neither sought a new livelihood, nor did he turn into the narrow intellectual or demagogic path envisaged and feared by his old friends as the only alternative. But he spent his time in his father's house, and continued in a resolute plan the wide reading which had already characterised his life. He became one of the great readers of the century, and one might even say that through his little study there flowed the whole stream of contemporary writing. His letters are full of his reading, and his writings reflect an immense range of interest. The Latin classics, especially Horace, the Church Fathers, Luther, modern work of every kind, and above all the Bible, filled his days. From 24 January to 8 April of 1781 he read through the 54 volumes of Voltaire's works. During these first years of the new life he became a philologian, reading, besides the languages he was already conversant with, in Greek, Hebrew and Arabic. They were perhaps the happiest years of his life. Yet he was jobless, and without any reasonably assured future. With far less worldly security than Kierkegaard, he turned aside with much simpler decisiveness from the idea of ordination. Another chance which offered itself, in an invitation from Christoph Friedrich Nicolai (1733-1811) of Berlin to join him in his literary projects, was also rejected. He was resolute in his opposition to the works of the " Nicolaitans," as he called them, playing on the happy similarity of the name to that of the obscure gnostic sect mentioned in the book of Revelation (2. 15). The tone of his life during this period is well illustrated by a remark in a letter of 13 June, 1760, to Lindner, where he speaks of his vast and intense reading as

> children's games which God has given me in order that the time till his appearing should not be long for me.[1]

Perhaps the lingering influence of pietism in the forms of his

[1] B II, 27.

thought account for the rather depreciatory tone of the reference to his reading. The eschatological strain remains all his days, and as we shall see dominates and transforms his views, and provides the unifying force for his entire thought. The mixture of influences appears in the collection of his writings which was published in 1762, including as it does the little masterpiece of eschatological imagination, *Die Magi aus Morgenlande*, as well as the *Kleeblatt Hellenistischer Briefe*, a series of studies, mainly philological, of classical and New Testament Greek, and the manifesto of the *Sturm und Drang*, the *Æsthetica in Nuce*. Even the title of the collection, *Kreuzzüge eines Philologen*, " Crusades of a Philologian," may also be translated simply as " Cross-currents."

In this same period Hamann's brother began to show signs of the disease which finally reduced him to complete melancholia. He too returned, from a teaching post, to his father's house. Their mother had died shortly before Hamann's departure for England. Now two new figures appear, who are to accompany Hamann all his life.

The first is Johann Gottfried Herder (1744-1803), one of the great figures of eighteenth century Germany, who came to Königsberg in 1762 as the protégé of a Russian medical officer (Königsberg was under Russian occupation from January 1758 till February 1763). He intended to study medicine, but soon turned to theology. He was just eighteen. With him Hamann quickly entered on a friendship which endured with only minor breaks for the rest of his life. This is the first of the friendships in which Hamann showed himself to be almost a genius; a good thing in itself, this friendship is at the same time of almost incalculable significance for Herder's own development, and through him for the whole new opening world of the *Sturm und Drang* and the Romantic movement in German life and letters. Their actual time together was very brief, for it is not clear that they became thoroughly acquainted immediately on Herder's arrival in Königsberg, and Herder left Königsberg for good in November 1764. Their letters are a precious source of European life and thought for the next crucial twenty years. Yet for the immediate purpose of watching the movement of Hamann's thought the later exchange of letters with Friedrich Heinrich Jacobi (1743-1819) is more manageable. Jacobi was a wealthy, warm-hearted Rhinelander, who lived a life of philosophic ease on his estate of Pempelfort near Düsseldorf. The ease was broken by his own Christian convictions, which led him out to tilt not only against Moses Mendelssohn, in a controversy about Spinoza, but also against Kant. Hamann did not always find it possible to agree with Jacobi's spirited but ill-managed defence of faith, but the relation between the two was warmer and more personal than the relation between Hamann and the more original spirit of Herder. When Hamann finally met Jacobi, during the last strange months of his life which were centred on Münster, it was with a feeling of relief on both sides that Hamann left Pempelfort for Münster again.

About the same time as Herder came to Königsberg, the second of the two new figures began to dominate Hamann's passions. This was Anna Regina Schumacher, a peasant girl who had entered his father's household at Easter 1762, and rapidly became to the ailing father almost as a daughter. She was twenty-four, and, as Hamann later described her, "of full-blooded and blooming health, and a just as robust and stupid honesty and stedfastness."[1] Within a few months he was writing to Nicolai in Berlin of "a left-handed marriage" with her. Why? Hamann's own explicit reason, from the same letter to Herder of 1776, why there was no official marriage, was

not because I am too proud, for I am too thankful, but because

[1] Letter to Herder, 15 October, 1776, B III, 262.

I am convinced that this situation [marriage] would lessen her own happiness, and could even be a disadvantage to her children.

Moreover—and here is perhaps the heart of the clue—as his officially acknowledged wife she would perhaps become " I know not what."[1] That is, if I understand a story in which silences play so large a part, Hamann feared that she might become a petty bourgeois creature. The reality of marriage—and there is no doubt that the reality was there, both in joys and sorrows—could only be preserved in circumstances which did not permit the intrusion of civil and ecclesiastical forms. An understanding of Hamann's attitude in this basic relation of his life, however difficult it was for the clergy of Königsberg and is for many to-day, is essential for the appreciation of his free, genuine and personal relation to existence. This is at the opposite extreme from the " arrogant life that is based upon civil and levitical righteousness,"[2] as he wrote to Lindner in February 1763. Here he is hinting at the remarkable part which faith plays in his practical decisions. The matter must be discussed again in the context of his whole understanding of faith. Later that year he took a job in the Royal Prussian Office of War and Property. The main lines of his life are now set. The attractive invitation from Friedrich Karl von Moser, that he should become tutor to the Princess of Hesse's eldest son, was rejected by Hamann mainly because he could not thus lightly abandon his " hamadryad," his " *Weib*," Anna Regina. Nevertheless he made a journey to Frankfurt in the summer of 1764, which turned out to be fruitless and ill-managed, as Moser did not happen to be at home.

From June 1765 till January 1767 he acted as a kind of secretary to a lawyer in Mitau, a friend from the Grünhof days. Legal

---

[1] Ibid., 263.   [2] 11 February, 1763, B II, 193.

business took them to Warsaw for five months. In Riga he had the opportunity of meeting Herder again, who was at that time at the cathedral school.

Though his father died in September 1766, it was not till January of 1767 that he returned to Königsberg. There, in May of the same year, he secured a job in the Customs office, through the kindly offices of Kommerzienrat G. C. R. Jacobi and Professor Immanuel Kant. It was his duty to translate into French all incoming German letters and documents—French being the official language of the immense bureaucracy which Frederick II had constructed for the management of his kingdom's affairs. Hamann's monthly salary was twenty-five talers. A year later he rented a house for fifty talers per annum. (A professor's salary at that time was anything from four hundred to eighteen hundred talers per annum, plus fees.) Anna Regina bore him his first child, Johann Michael, in September 1769. In 1770 he bought for 1,000 gulden (plus 1,000 in extras) a house of his own, where he lived till, in 1777, with promotion, he got an official house. Here in the first house of his own his independent and fruitful years were spent. Here he learned to eat his bread and drink his wine with gladness. Here he gulped down the caviare which his friend and publisher Hartknoch of Riga sent him, and with equal appetite devoured the books which poured into his house. Here he penned the immense and lively letters, sometimes detailed like Dutch interiors, sometimes brilliant with light at one point like a Rembrandt, sometimes simply swarming with life, without any ulterior motive, like a Brueghel village scene. For Hamann made no distinction between his public and private life, whether as author, Customs official, family man or friend. From here he went daily to his ill-paid but not onerous duties as a taxgatherer in the service of Frederick the Great, the type for Hamann of all that was false and inhuman in the life of the Enlightenment. Here too he rose before the dawn to write articles and help to edit Kanter's journal, the *Königsbergsche Gelehrte und Politische Zeitungen*. These labours went on till 1776, nor can it be said that Hamann was unhappy in them. In a letter of 11 February, 1763 to Lindner he spoke of his own possibilities quite candidly:

School and academic work are not for me, since I cannot really lecture [partly, at least, on account of his " thick tongue "]; nor is anything right for me that demands legal learning and abstract conception. To be just a copyist would harm my eyes and go against my health and inclination. All that is left is the Mint, the Customs, and the Excise. The Customs would be my choice.[1]

The nadir in Hamann's worldly affairs was reached in 1776, when he felt obliged for the sake of his four children, whom (as he said in a letter to the General Administration asking for leave of absence) " je vois périr faute d'éducation," to auction his library of over two thousand volumes. This was simultaneously the moment when Herder's friendship was expressed in its most concrete form. Herder by a splendid fiction of applying a mortgage on the books (by which he became co-owner) averted what could only have meant death for Hamann—the loss of his books. Thereafter his affairs, though never really free from embarrassment, became tolerable. In 1784 he received from a young Westphalian landowner, Franz Buchholtz, a gift of 4,000 talers for the education of his children. A first meeting with his benefactor was only possible in 1787, when after many delays and vexations he finally received, not leave of absence, as he had wished, but his dismissal from the post of manager of the Customs warehouse (to which he had been promoted in 1777), a dismissal couched in curt and mocking terms which are a little classic of bureaucratic spite.

So Hamann set out in the summer of 1787 on his last journey,

[1] B II, 191.

from which he was not to return. Buchholtz was at Wellbergen, Jacobi at Pempelfort, and the Princess Amalie von Gallitzin at Angelmodde. This remarkable constellation of figures, which included Franz Hemsterhuis (1722-90) the Dutch philosopher, half Platonist, half pantheist, Franz Freiherr von Fürstenberg (1728-1810), the prince-bishop's vicar general in Münster, and Bernard Overberg, another Roman Catholic priest, has been described as the "Münster circle." In truth there was here a remarkable grouping of individuals, each of whom had an independent significance. So far as Hamann was concerned, the months meant primarily the rapid, intense, fine and unspoiled blossoming of a late friendship with the Princess Gallitzin, the fuller significance of which is discussed later. The records, from Hamann's letters and the Princess's diaries, describe most explicitly a situation as rare as it is desirable; the meeting of persons in utter openness, without consideration of standpoints which have to be maintained or attitudes which have to be struck. Those who try to prove that the Princess Gallitzin, a devout Roman Catholic, was on the way to Wittenberg, or that Hamann, a Lutheran *pur sang*, was on the way to Rome, do not understand the inwardness and the liberating power of a conviction, intensely held, and, because of that very intensity, open to the fresh wind of the Spirit.

It was in this situation, in which the Spirit blew about his life in a remarkable power of benediction, that Hamann's overtaxed body finally yielded; and on 21 June, 1788, in the house of Franz Buchholtz, he died.

3

FAITH

On 17 April, 1757 Johann Georg Hamann arrived at Harwich by the packet-boat from Helvoetsluys in Holland. He was twenty-seven years of age, and a native of the thriving international port of Königsberg. Behind him lay six years of unfinished studies at the university, and some five years with various families in Livonia and Courland as a house-tutor. His situation was like that of countless young men of that time, of some talent but of no means. He always maintained a lively interest in teaching, as various writings testify—especially the letters to Kant regarding the writing of a physics book for children, which Kant had proposed they should collaborate in producing. The scheme did not survive Hamann's letters to Kant.[1] At a later date his own son, Hans Michael, was to be well on with his Greek at the age of ten, and about to start on Hebrew. He survived to become a teacher in the grammar school at Königsberg.

Now one of Hamann's great longings, common indeed to many young Germans of the day, to be in England, was being fulfilled.

It was the England of the classical age, the Enlightenment: moulded in taste by the *Spectator* and the *Tatler*, by the verse of Pope and the magniloquent periods of the *Rambler*; moulded theologically by a great desire for peace and rational accommodation, even when the deistic assertions concerning a happily remote control of human affairs by the Deity were by no means

[1] See below, 238ff.

39

always acceptable in their extreme forms; and moulded in thought by Bacon and Locke and David Hume, with their empirical, sense-bound philosophy, more modest than the mathematical rationalism of Christian Wolff in Germany, who wanted, as he said, to bring mathematical certainty to religious propositions. We have no evidence that Hamann met any of the literary personages of London at that time, though his wide, intense and unflagging interest in English writing undoubtedly dates from the time of his stay in London. Indeed, in his London autobiography he speaks, in the fervour of his conversion, of having bought " two suits of clothes, the waistcoat of one pretty richly bedecked, and a mass of books." We know, too, that the ground for this continuing interest had already been prepared during his time as a house-tutor, when he writes in various letters of Young, Hervey and Hume. Young's *Conjectures on Original Composition*, which had such a profound effect on Hamann and his younger German contemporaries, did not appear till 1759; but the *Night Thoughts* had appeared by 1745, and Hervey's *Meditations and Contemplations* in 1746-47. And Hume's thought was to occupy Hamann all his days.[1]

But Hamann was commissioned by his friends and employers of the Berens family, merchants in Riga, for other purposes. What precisely these were it is hard to say. All that we know for certain is that they involved the Russian embassy, and combined political and commercial interests. The commission was secret, and Hamann kept the secret well. What we know of his London sojourn, which lasted till June 1758—fourteen months in all—is derived from his own writings of that time, chiefly from the *Thoughts about my Life*, *Biblical Reflections*, and *Fragments*.

In brief, what Hamann learned in London was that the way for him lay through " a descent into hell, the hell of self-

[1] Cf. B I, 140, 199, 127.

knowledge," as he later described it, " which is the only way to being one with God (Vergötterung)."[1] In London he underwent a conversion of an intensity which marked his whole life. But it was not of the kind which petrified into a dated event in his past or into a static platitude. The change which took place in him during his London experience involved a twofold break: on the one hand with the pietist leanings derived from his home, and on the other hand with the rationalist influences which surrounded him in the university. His writings of the time still betray marks of his pietist upbringing, but he was more and more to leave these behind as the full force of the change expressed itself in his thought and his decisions. And the veiled rationalism of a philosopher like Martin Knutzen did not appear to Hamann to be the real enemy to his way of life. For the blend of pietism and Wolffian rationalism in Knutzen's thought concealed from Hamann for a time that the break involved every kind of rationalism.

Positively, we may say that Hamann's London experience meant a dynamic assertion of his own existence as lived in the presence of God's Word. And this assertion persisted throughout his life, gradually taking over every area of his interests and his thoughts until no part of his life was left untouched.

What was the precise nature of the change? Tumultuous, certainly; grounded on an intense, reiterated, highly individual reading of the whole Bible, not once, but twice through, the New Testament even three times; and taking him through absolute despair in himself to absolute confidence in the Lord of the Word, which involved (though this was only gradually to become evident) " a completely primitive and simple relation to life."[2]

The motto to his Biblical Reflections, which he wrote during this time, begins as follows:

[1] R II, 198 = N II, 164.   [2] Cf. T. Schack, Hamann, Copenhagen, 1948, 14.

All biblical history is a prophecy which is fulfilled in every century and in the soul of man.[1]

This supplies the key to an understanding of Hamann's attitude: he read the Bible as a way to the understanding of himself. It was his own fate that was spread before him in the history of the children of Israel, both in judgment and in promise. I give the climax of the story in his own words:

I recognised my own crimes in the history of the Jewish people. I read the course of my own life, and thanked God for his long-suffering with this people, since nothing but such an example could justify me in a like hope. Above all, in the books of the Law I found a remarkable disclosure, that the Israelites, however crude they appear to us, nevertheless in some instances sought from God nothing but what he was willing to do for them; that they acknowledged their disobedience in as lively a way as any repentant sinner ever did, and forgot their penitence just as quickly; but that in their fear they called for nothing else but a Redeemer, an Advocate, a Mediator, without whom they could neither fear nor love God aright. With these reflections, which seemed to me very mysterious, in the evening of 31 March I read the fifth chapter of Deuter-onomy, and fell into deep thought. I thought of Abel, of whom God said, The earth has opened her mouth to receive thy brother's blood. —I felt my heart thump, I heard a voice sigh in its depths and wail like the voice of blood, like the voice of a slain brother who wanted to avenge his blood if I did not hear it betimes and went on stopping my ears to it—saying that it was just this which made Cain a wanderer and a fugitive. All at once I felt my heart swell, and pour out

---

[1] R I, 50 (but this Motto appears in Nadler's edition at N I, 315, as the opening sentence of *Reflections upon Newton's Treatment of the Prophecies*).

in tears, and I could no longer—I could no longer conceal from my God that I was the fratricide, the murderer of his only begotten Son. The Spirit of God went on, in spite of my great weakness, and the long resistance I had made against his witness and his stirring of me, to reveal to me more and more the mystery of the divine love and the benefit of faith in our gracious and only Saviour.[1]

In this way Hamann entered into and became a part of the story he was reading. The old history was " re-enacted," to use Collingwood's phrase,[2] but not merely in his understanding or even his feelings and imagination, but in his whole being. " All the miracles of Holy Scripture take place in our soul," he said.[3] It is a return to himself, an end to the flight from himself, which he describes so vividly in the whole autobiography and which culminates in the London crisis. He himself is fully engaged in the history he finds in the Bible. He came to himself, and accepted what he was. This did not mean the acceptance of a new harmony. On the contrary, it meant a final and decisive break with the conception of a harmonious life in a harmonious universe which was characteristic of the rationalism of the time. Nor did it mean, as with the pietists, the entry into a special domain of religion. In London, then, Hamann broke in principle simultaneously with the philosophy of the Enlightenment and with the specialism of Pietism. From that time his life was determined as one which was to be lived in existence as a whole: not, that is to say, merely in conceptions, or the understanding, as an observer of interesting phenomena, far less in a separated realm of religious exercises and emotions: but in a direct relation to existence. This does not mean that he abandoned any effort to understand what his faith meant; nor that he cut himself from the ordinary

[1] R I, 212f. = N II, 40f.
[2] R. G. Collingwood, *The Idea of History*, 215ff., 282ff.
[3] *Biblical Reflections*, R I, 83 = N I, 78.

life of the church. Rather, his whole life is an effort to understand his faith as something that determines his life; and this effort leads him, not into isolation, but into the cultivation of the society of God and his neighbour. Solitude, and a sense of being an exception, and misunderstood or ignored, certainly characterised his whole life.[1] But these are characteristics of all lives of creative freedom.

The positive significance of Hamann's new position only gradually became apparent. But it cannot be restricted, as is often done, and given a merely negative form. Hamann is more than a prophet of irrationalism[2], and more than an advocate of the feelings.[3] Tertullian is not his master, and Schleiermacher, as conventionally understood, not his true follower. For Hamann was as much a critic of the Romantic movement—in the sense that he was much less one-sided in his æsthetic than his immediate heirs among the German Romantics, however strong his emphasis on the life of the senses and passions—as he was its obvious precursor and instigator. Professor John Macmurray, in the first volume of his Gifford Lectures,[4] recognises the significance of Hamann not only as an opponent of the Critical philosophy of Kant, but also as standing at the beginning of the whole new Romantic movement in art and philosophy. He describes him as " the founder of the Faith philosophy," which involves the recognition that " we can know reality only by means of faith." When he goes on to describe this faith as being " in radical

---

[1] See, as one example for many, R II, 239 = N II, 187: " Evangelical truth should therefore not blush at the ostracism which banishes the sweetness, salt and savour of its speech from the best society."

[2] R. Unger, *Hamann und die Aufklärung*, Jena, 1911, I, 115, calls Hamann " an irrationalist and therefore an anti-rationalist," and it is this pervading judgment which makes Unger's great study in the last resort incapable of discerning the radical newness of Hamann's position.

[3] A typical assessment of this kind may be found in H. Hettner, *Geschichte der deutschen Literatur im 18. Jahrhundert*, Leipzig, 1909, 3. I, 270, where Hamann is described as being at the head of " a new pietistic literature," fleeing from " thought into the realms of the life of feeling."

[4] *The Self as Agent*, London, 1957, 41ff.

opposition to reason," and to define it as "our capacity for æsthetic experience," he certainly makes an advance on the common classification of Hamann simply as an irrationalist or a *Gefühlsphilosoph*, a "philosopher of feeling." But it is doubtful to me whether a full study of Hamann's views can substantiate either the simple disjunction, and opposition, between faith and reason, on the one hand, or the restriction, on the other hand, of the activity of faith to the intuition of the artist. Reason is not the enemy of faith, nor is faith to be understood as an immediate, as opposed to a discursive, grasp of reality.

The difficulty here, in describing the positive nature of the change in Hamann, and its consequences for his whole life and activity, is on a par with the difficulty which Hamann found in expressing himself. For the problem is both larger, and more intense, than the comparatively simple matter of the history of ideas and influences among artists and philosophers. It is really the paradox of Christian existence which lies in the heart of the matter. In the last resort this paradox is not capable of expression in terms of exposition, either from the head or from the heart. It is not capable of being subsumed in doctrines, or described as an immediate response to reality. It is not even capable of being expressed in the completeness of a life. In the *Concluding Unscientific Postscript* Kierkegaard speaks of "the individual, by an internal decision, putting an end to mere possibility, and identifying himself with the content of his thought in order to exist in it."[1] This internal decision is a decision of faith, which leaps into the possibilities of thought and transforms them into existence. We have to do here neither with an epistemology nor with an æsthetic, but with a decision which includes a relation—in traditional terminology, a relation with God as the Word. And the consequence of this venture is neither a harmonious system nor a transparent life. But the consequence is a witnessing

[1] E.T., 302.

individual. And this is what Hamann called himself, " a wooden signpost,"[1] pointing the way which each individual must go for himself.

The immediate consequence of these decisions for Hamann himself was his return home. He finally reached Königsberg again in January 1759. From that time his whole life is to be understood as a long-drawn-out lesson in humility, in self-humiliation springing from self-knowledge. Consequently, there is little external incident to relate, and of success of his life there is nothing at all to relate. He abandoned what prospects he may have had in a commercial career with his Riga friends. He broke with Berens who had sent him to London. And he resolved to undertake the care of his ailing father—his mother had died before he left for London. This course of action meant at the same time a break with the presuppositions of his whole environment. He could no longer be the normal man of the Enlightenment, conforming to the principles, ideals and norms of the time. He embarked upon a life of faith, which meant that he had to be an exception.

In a long and fantastic letter to Kant, dated 27 July, 1759,[2] he makes the break with Berens, and incidentally with Kant himself, as clear as it could be made. Kant had been drawn in by Berens to try to persuade Hamann not to be foolish, and not to withdraw into what seemed to both Berens and Kant to be pious obscurantism. The letter symbolises the relationship, which is much more than a nodding acquaintanceship, yet hardly to be described as friendship, which persisted between Hamann and Kant for more than a quarter of a century. It is a remarkable token to Kant's forbearance, and to Hamann's love of genuineness, that the two should have succeeded in meeting one another on any

[1] " I can do no more than the arm of a signpost, and am too wooden to accompany my readers in the course of their reflections," R II, 38 = N II, 76. Cf. letter to Jacobi, 14 December, 1785, G 158: " At least I will stretch out my wooden arm as far as I can, to show the right way to those who are able to grasp it."
[2] R I, 429-445 = B I, 373-381. See also 238ff, below.

level at all. In all their relations there is a curious mingling of mutual respect, exasperation, and even incomprehension. On one occasion, when asking Hamann for his views on his (Kant's) analysis of Herder's *Die Älteste Urkunde des Menschengeschlechts*, Kant besought Hamann to write " in human language. Poor son of earth that I am, I am not organised to understand the divine language of the intuitive reason."[1]

In this letter Hamann is indeed attempting to show Kant the meaning of a different language and life from his own: a language which is not bound by the law of contradiction, because it reflects a life which is itself a unity of opposites, a *coincidentia oppositorum*.[2] Everything, he says, depends on the eyes with which one sees, and the place from which one sees:

> When two men are in different positions, they must never dispute about their sense-impressions. A watcher in an observatory has much to tell to one who is in the third story. The latter must not be so stupid as to say that the watcher's eyes are defective. " Come down, and you will be convinced that you have seen nothing." A man in a deep ditch where there is no water can see the stars at noon. The man on the surface does not deny the stars, but he can only see the lord of the day . . .

But Hamann's effort to explain his position to Kant was, I think, bound to fail. From Kant's point of view the letter was a piece of self-willed folly, which could lead nowhere.[3] It is a

---

[1] In a letter of 6 April, 1774, B III, 82.

[2] Though Hamann found this principle of immense use, he wrongly attributed it to Giordano Bruno (cf N III, 107), and did not know the work of Nicolas Cusanus. Cf. also letter to Herder, 17 November, 1782: " Bruno's *principium coincidentiæ oppositorum* is worth more in my eyes than all Kantian critique."

[3] Hegel calls the letters to Kant among " the liveliest, most open and comprehensible " of all Hamann's writings (op. cit., 221). But this is not to say that Kant understood them, or the impulse behind them, or the life whose style was being established during this time of struggle. Nor indeed does Hegel, for all the vigour and penetration of his account, understand that at this decisive time in his life Hamann simply cannot be judged by the standards applicable to a " useful " citizen, with a proper job and a corresponding spiritual

manifesto of Christian existence over against the spinning of
abstractions which even at this early stage Hamann thought he
could detect in Kant. He and Kant had a different understanding
of what truth is. For Hamann everything depended upon the
individual and his place in existence and in the moment, and this
meant that man by himself is unfinished. " Man by himself is a
question needing an answer, an emptiness waiting to be filled."[1]
Man exists only in relation with God and his neighbour and with
the life of nature in the midst of which he is set.[2] It is God who
makes out of our present moment something perfect and
complete, revealing both the past and the future to us. He alone
is the Lord of time.[3] So for Hamann the individual is not one
who is called, and able, to move towards some kind of finish
and perfection, by submitting to the view of the normal man
which dominates the Enlightenment. The truth about man lies
for Hamann in man's boundary situation, where he cries, with
the Psalmist, " I am a worm and no man."[4] But this fearful
self-knowledge, which, as he says, unites in human life " every-

---

conformity, and propriety. In fact, Hegel's standpoint is as interesting for letting us see
where *he* stands as where he thinks Hamann stands. As one illustration of this, the
criticism that Hamann was filled with hatred for the public for whom he writes (op.
cit. 254) rests on a double misapprehension: Hamann did not write for " the public "
but for the individual (whom, in relation to the public, he calls " nobody "); and he
did not hate his readers.

[1] Schack, op. cit., 206.,

[2] Cf. *Fragments*, R I, 139-142 = N I, 304-5.

[3] Cf. *Biblical Reflections*, R I, 90 = N I, 125-6, and 131 below.

[4] R III, 253f. = N IV, 282. The context of the quotation is as follows: " ' I am a
worm and no man '; these feelings of the royal psalmist seem to be the only signposts
for reaching the desired idea of the majesty of existence. The marks of revelation should
not be compared with the type of a metaphysical idol but with the open and great
mystery of a Word become flesh; and an exposition of Christian ethics should have as
its object not the morality of actions but *the holiness of life*; for with all propriety of a
good state you can by no means presuppose love of virtue, and with love of virtue you
can by no means presuppose rebirth and the new creature. . . . Morality of actions seems
to be a standard for works righteousness rather than for a life hidden with Christ in God.
In the following of Jesus, who learned obedience and fulfilment through suffering,
consists the fulness of all virtues. . . ." Cf. also R IV, 41 = N III, 38: " No hero or poet,
whether a type of the Messiah or a prophet of anti-Christ, lacks periods in his life when
he has every reason to confess with David, ' I am a worm and no man.' "

thing that can make the day terrible and the night fearful,"[1] is not a simple knowledge, leading to death. It is a dialectical knowledge, born in contradiction and tension, but it leads to life.

Many years later, in a letter to Herder of 3 June, 1781, he writes:

This fear in the world [like Noah in his ark] is the sole proof of our heterogeneity. For if we lacked nothing we would not be any better than the heathen and the transcendental philosophers, who know nothing of God, and become enamoured of dear Nature like fools; no homesickness would assail us. This irrelevant unrest, this holy hypochondria, is perhaps the fire with which we beasts of sacrifice must be salted and preserved from the corruption of the present age.[2]

Therefore it is man's earth-boundness which is at the same time the way leading to a knowledge of his difference, his heterogeneity. And out of this knowledge, both of his difference and of his incompleteness, the Christian discerns his destiny.

The Christian alone is a man, a father, lord of the animals. He alone loves himself, his own and his goods, because he loves God who loved him before he was . . . The Christian alone is lord of his days, because he is heir to the future.[3]

For Kant it may be said that virtue and beauty lie in man himself. But for Hamann man is entirely dependent upon what he receives from outside himself:

On a better understanding our dignity depends not on our own mind, will, or activity, but is the gift of a higher choice, not an inborn merit but one which is acquired, but not acquired through oneself, not independent, but simply dependent

[1] R I, 96 = N I, 146-7. [2] R VI, 194.
[3] R I, 80 = N I, 71 (but Roth is incomplete).

(*schlechterdings abhängiges*), and for that reason the firmer and more immovable.[1]

So Hamann's presupposition for truth is faith. In faith alone can he be sustained in the recognition of his sin and nothingness before God, and at the same time be enabled to live a life of freedom and of love for his fellow-men.

In the same letter to Kant, Hamann writes:

> Reason is not given to you in order that you may become wise, but that you may know your folly and ignorance; as the Mosaic law was not given to the Jews to make them righteous, but to make their sins more sinful to them.

This description certainly involves an attack upon the Enlightenment view of the nature and capacities of reason. But it is more important positively than negatively. That is, it is not so much a simple attack upon the capacities of reason as a sign of Hamann's quickened conception of what faith is. He takes his start from Hume, whom he quotes at length in the same letter, as the thinker who in his view has best seen the place of faith in man's life. He quotes the famous passage on miracles from the *Enquiry concerning Human Understanding*, prefacing it with the remark that "a man may preach the truth against his will and knowledge, in jest." The passage is as follows:

> So that, upon the whole, we may conclude, that the Christian religion not only was at first attended with miracles, but even at this day cannot be believed by any reasonable person without one. Mere reason is insufficient to convince us of its veracity. And whoever is moved by Faith to assent to it, is conscious of

[1] R VII, 287, letter to Scheffner, 18 September, 1785. It is interesting to note that Schleiermacher, in introducing in his *Glaubenslehre* the key phrase of "absolute dependence" (*schlechthinige Abhängigkeit*), acknowledges his debt to Delbrück. and adds: "I am not aware that it [*schlechthinig*] has occurred anywhere else." But a word very like it is here used by H., and the idea is basic to H.'s views. If only Schleiermacher had read Hamann more attentively!

a continued miracle in his own person, which subverts all the
principles of his understanding, and gives him a determination
to believe what is most contrary to custom and experience.[1]

It is doubtful whether by belief Hume meant at all what
Hamann meant by faith. Belief for Hume was rather an attitude
of mind which carried the mind in and through the world of the
senses to the " independently real." Certainly in this passage one
receives the impression that Hume is mocking as openly as ever
he did in his published works. Because the Christian religion can
only be believed with the aid of miracles, therefore (he implies),
it does not really enter into the province of any sensible man.
For Hume's mind, at least, Christianity had ceased to be a live
option—though it was a different matter where his " feeling "
was concerned.

For Hamann the opposite conclusion is true. He takes Hume's
own argument, and re-asserts faith as the only possible response.
He regards reason as leading him to the limits of human possibility, that is, to the point where the mind admits that it knows, is
faced with, nothing. For Hume this is the point of resignation
and return. For Hamann it is the point of departure. This is
something very different from the radical opposition between
reason and faith which is commonly associated with Hamann's
name. It is also something different from the scholastic compromise between the respective provinces and capacities of reason and
faith—different mainly, as we shall see, because of the different
significance seen in the limits of reason's capacities and because
of the different weight put upon the actual activity of faith.
When he says that the function of reason is to be a schoolmaster
for faith,[2] there is a formal resemblance with the medieval
position. And when he seizes on the superficial concession which

[1] op. cit., Sect. X, II, 101.
[2] His exact words are, " The function of philosophy is Moses in person, an Orbilius
for faith." R II, 101, note.

51

Hume makes to belief, he might seem to be merely making the best of a bad job. But the way in which he both respects[1] and yet goes beyond Hume's position (both his intellectual position and the silent compromise of his actual conduct) indicates that Hamann is pointing to a new possibility, which neither the scholastics nor the *illuminati* were able to see. He deepens the conception of faith so that the disjunction between it and reason is in a fair way to being overcome, in the unity of his existence.

This deepened conception of faith may be seen at work both in his life and in his writings. The decision to care for his father in his declining years, and also for his brother, who gradually sank into complete melancholia, and lived on till 1778 in Hamann's small and crowded house, indicates the way he was going: not the way of a harmonious and successful life, but the way of renunciation and humility.

But this return home meant also a new beginning. It is typified in his first proper published work, the *Socratic Memorabilia*.

This short work, which was published in 1759, and consists of some thirty-three pages in the modern edition, I shall not try to summarise here—even if a summary were possible at all.[2] One writer has said of him, " he thought as those who do not think would think if they were to think."[3] This judgment is not intended as a comment upon Hamann's obscurity, but as praise, in so far as Hamann, like the unthinking, does not reach his goal by means of discursive thought, but by a certain robust and obstinate personal assertion, whether of intuition or of faith. But at the same time it must be added that a prejudice in favour of his style is almost a pre-requisite for making anything of the content. It is a style in which the man and his experiences are

---

[1] In a letter to Herder, 10 May, 1781, he writes: " Hume is always my man, because he at least honours the principle of belief, and has taken it into his system. Our country-man [Kant] keeps on chewing the cud of Hume's fury against causality, without taking this matter of belief into account. That does not seem to me to be honest."

[2] See below, 175ff.

[3] J. Blum, *La Vie et l'œuvre de J.-G. Hamann*, Paris, 1912, 48.

perpetually spilling over the edges of his art; a style which, if successful, marks the end of classicism, and a call to a fresh reliance on originality, on the passions, and on genius.

Hamann himself speaks, in one of the two prefaces to the *Socratic Memorabilia*, of the work being comprehensible only to " readers who can swim," consisting as it does of " many little islands unconnected either by bridge or ferry in its method." In other words, we have here not so much an argument as a series of aphorisms, connected not by the author's logical powers but by the reader's complaisance, like-mindedness, and willingness to respond.

In brief, Hamann here flings down the gauge against both the style and the presuppositions of his time. To do this he makes use of the figure of Socrates. His knowledge of Plato at the time seems to have been extremely perfunctory, and later he mentions, in a letter to Jacobi, that he was " full of Hume " when he wrote the *Socratic Memorabilia*.[1] Nevertheless, Socrates becomes the focal point for Hamann's " genial and ironically superior and yet desperately serious declaration of war upon the spirit of his age."[2] But it is only superficially that Hamann, by making use of Socrates as his central figure, departs from the intensely personal and inward concern which came to light in the London experience and in the London writings. In the *Socratic Memorabilia* as in the *Reflections* and *Thoughts* the chief concern is a summons to self-knowledge, in opposition to the norms of the age which aimed chiefly at making men conform and be " serviceable."

The choice of Socrates for his purpose meant three things. First, it meant that faith for Hamann is of the same order as Socratic ignorance. But this is only the beginning. This ignorance is not final. For Hume, who, as we know, was much in Hamann's mind at the time, and who may be taken as typical of the best of the time, one can I think say that belief is at most a psychological

[1] G 506, letter of 27 April, 1787.   [2] R. Unger, op. cit., 10.

necessity, which provides unverifiable knowledge about the connections of things. Belief for Hume is therefore a final resignation. But for Hamann faith is the form of truth. It is not merely a probability, depending upon the criterion of custom and conformity. Indeed, in reaction against this Humian position, Hamann can even propose this paradoxical statement for the form of faith: " Lies and novels, hypotheses and fables, must be probable; but not the truths and basic teachings of our faith."[1] Truth is not to be measured by human opinions, or taste, or probability.

It is doubtful whether this view can be shown to depend upon the Platonic Socrates. There are several possible interpretations of what the Platonic Socrates really stands for, as Philip Merlan has pointed out recently.[2] But it is doubtful whether we are justified in seeing him, with Hamann, as " the climax of what natural reason, unaided by Christian revelation, can and should attain, insight into its own insufficiency and groping after the concept of sin."[3] Socrates's ignorance may be more simply understood as a technique for reaching knowledge rather than as a movement of resignation of all rational knowledge. And in fact another great stream of interpretation (as Merlan also points out) is that which sees Socrates as one of the great teachers of natural religion. In other words, it is doubtful whether Hamann really grasped all that Socrates stood for. But it is also clear that Hamann did find in Socrates the same personal movement towards the truth which for Hamann himself is expressed in faith.

This comes out most clearly in the second point of affinity between Hamann and Socrates. For Hamann faith means the encounter of the whole man through self-knowledge with the living truth of the Spirit. " Flesh and blood are hypotheses, the

---

[1] R I, 425 = B I, 359, a letter to his brother, 16 July, 1759.
[2] In an essay, " Form and Content in Plato's Philosophy," *Journal of the History of Ideas*, VIII, 4.
[3] Ibid. 416, n. 33.

spirit is truth," he writes. Surely here there is a real affinity with Socrates, with his intensely personal relation to the truth, and his sense of being in the care of his genius. Hamann and Socrates are here alike in that neither professed a doctrine, but " existed " in their philosophising.

Thirdly, in the mode of his expression Hamann follows Socrates. The sense of the insufficiency of reason and the sense of being guided by a higher power in a personal way combine to produce a distinctive style which can be summarised as constituted of indirectness, of irony above all, and of the humility which makes a real acknowledgment of the limits of knowledge. This is the very opposite of the arrogance of the sceptic, of whom Hamann says, " He who needs so much quickness and eloquence to convince himself of his own ignorance must have in his heart an immense opposition to the truth of his ignorance."[1]

For Hamann, then, Socratic ignorance is the ante-room to faith. This ignorance he further describes as *Empfindung* (which Schack translates as *Erfaring*, German *Erfahrung*, experience),[2] which is perhaps best translated as sensibility, with the connotation of experiencing by means of the senses. Not therefore a knowledge of general truths, which can be built into a system and presented as theoretical and universally valid knowledge, and not an imaginative representation of something, which is based on an intuitive perception, but a recognition of your real existence, beyond reason and imagination, is what constitutes for Hamann the ignorance which leads to faith. This is an existential ignorance, and not merely, so to speak, a quantitative or statistical ignorance. We may draw out its positive significance by saying that at the limit of the mind's possibilities there comes into play a confident engagement of the whole person. Here faith comes into its own. " What one believes has for that reason no need to be proved, and a proposition can be irrefutably proved

[1] R II, 35 = N II, 73. [2] Op. cit., 103.

without for that reason being believed ... Faith is not a work of reason and therefore cannot succumb to any attack by reason; because believing happens as little by means of reasons as tasting and seeing."[1]

So we may say that for Hamann to have faith means to exist in ignorance. While it is therefore possible to agree with the judgment of Metzke that this "'ignorance' is not an affair of the *ratio* of knowing," it is misleading to go on, as he does, to say that it "can only come from the heart and is solely and wholly an affair of the heart and therefore a 'faith'."[2] This ignorance is rather a movement of the whole existence which is concentrated by means of the sensibility upon the opening possibilities of a life of faith. Ignorance is therefore not to be defined as the merely negative recognition of boundaries to knowledge, but as the positive recognition of the reality of existence. Existence is what is given to me, it is everything outside me, that which by being received, by speaking to me, by claiming me, brings me in turn into existence. As Metzke rightly says, Hamann is really thinking of a completely new relation of being, "which is not based on the *ratio*, but on the recognition of the order of being as God's order of creation, which does not mean an arbitrary taking for oneself, but the acceptance of what is given by God (for 'a man cannot take anything that is not given to him')."[3]

---

[1] R II, 36 = N II, 73-4.

[2] E. Metzke, *J. G. Hamanns Stellung in der Philosophie des 18. Jahrhunderts*, Halle, 1934, 191.

[3] Cf. G 377, R VII = N III, 377 and also, of course, the source of the Hamann quotation, in John 3. 27: "A man can receive nothing, except it be given him from heaven"; Metzke, op. cit., 180. I read his book only after completing this essay, but forbear to add too many references to it. I find myself in very close accord with Metzke's interpretation; only I find in Hamann's understanding of the Word, of faith and history—and indeed of all major topics of Christian interest—a more remarkable eschatological strain than Metzke does. For instance, on pp. 207-211 Metzke speaks of Hamann's view of "reality as wholeness." He rightly sees Hamann's view as being distinct from Kant's (and Hegel's), which is a *logical* wholeness, and from Herder's which is an *organic* (I should say, more precisely, an æsthetic) wholeness. Hamann's view is thoroughly Christian. But Metzke limits this conception of Christian to the sense of the connectedness of all creation. I should say that Hamann sees more: it is the making all things new, as a hope arising out of faith, which controls his thought. This goes farther than an ontology derived

It is in this context, of the recognition of existence as something given, which we accept and to which we respond, that Hamann launches his attack upon the whole scheme of rational demonstrations and proofs. " Our own being and the existence of all things outside us must be believed, and cannot be established in any other way."[1] Later he was to write the famous words taken up by Kierkegaard and so often wrongly attributed as original coinage to such modern theologians as Emil Brunner and Paul Tillich: " If it is fools who say in their heart. There is no God, those who try to prove his existence seem to me to be even more foolish."[2]

In the words of a shrewd observer of the time, J. H. Merck, Paymaster General of Hesse-Darmstadt, and a friend of Goethe,

> Now we have got the freedom of believing in public nothing but what can be rationally demonstrated. They have deprived religion of its sensuous elements, that is, of all its relish. They have carved it up into parts and reduced it to a skeleton without colour and light . . . and now it's put in a jar, and nobody wants to taste it.[3]

It was against this reduction of faith to the bounds of rational demonstration and its identification with its rationally demonstrable elements that Hamann fought all his life. There were in consequence occasions when he could speak with the utmost scorn and hatred of reason, as for instance in the highly charged but very obscure treatise *Conxompax*, where, in a polemic directed mainly against free-masonry, but also against the whole arrogation to itself by reason of eternal and universal truths, he writes:

---

from a view of reality as *created*. Being is rather grasped in its wholeness when seen as fulfilment in God, *i.e.*, eschatological fulfilment. And what applies to being applies also to history. (Cf. 93f below, and R VII, 57 = N III, 311; R VI, 44 = N II, 242; R II, 489 = N II, 261.)

[1] R II, 35 = N II, 73.   [2] G 230.
[3] From the *Teutsche Merkur*, 1779, quoted in Pascal, op. cit., 88.

For what is highly-praised reason, with its generalities, infallibil-ity, exuberance, certainty, and evidence? An *ens rationis*, an idol, to which divine attributes are ascribed by a blatant superstition of unreason.[1]

But on the whole he is clear that reason, like the law for the Jews, is holy and good. It is the *unreasonableness* of the claims for reason which strike him most forcibly. Thus in a letter written about the same time as the *Socratic Memorabilia*, to his life-long friend J. G. Lindner, he says:

> Our reason is therefore just what Paul calls the law—and the command of reason is holy, righteous and good. But is reason given to us to make us wise? As little as the law was given to the Jews to make them righteous, but to convince us of the opposite, how unreasonable our reason is, and that our errors must increase through it, as sin increased through the law. Let us, wherever Paul speaks of the law, put the law of our century and the watchword of our wise men, and our scribes, namely, the reason. So Paul will speak to our contemporaries . . .[2]

For just as reason, *Vernunft*, comes from *vernehmen*, to perceive, receive, so " our reason must wait and hope, and wish to be servant and not lawgiver to nature."[3] So he can also say, " without reason, no religion,"[4] for without reason there could be no recognition of limits, there could not be what Kierkegaard calls the " metaphysical dizziness " which is the portal to faith.

To sum up, faith for Hamann is on the one hand not an appendage of, or inferior substitute for reason, nor is it on the other hand divorced from the true exercise of reason. Reason, that is to say, is not autonomous over against faith. But reason

---

[1] R VI, 16 = N III, 225.   [2] R I, 405-6 = B I 355-6, letter of 3 July, 1759.
[3] G 16, 14 November, 1784.
[4] R VI, 25 = N III, 231 (cf. R VII, 9 = N III, 286).

can become (to use Tillich's word) " theonomous," that is, the bearer or vehicle of faith. It is not a separate and hostile element; but in and through the exercise of reason the possibility of faith appears. This does not mean, however, that faith is to be understood simply as the logical consequence of reason exercising its intrinsic possibilities. " Faith needs reason, as reason needs faith," he wrote much later to Jacobi.[1]

So faith cannot be understood as a simple and undialectical concept. It is certainty, but certainty in ignorance. It is ignorance, but ignorance leading to self-knowledge. And self-knowledge is taken up in being known. The whole basis of faith is *Empfindung*, the reception of impressions and experiences from outside ourselves. It is therefore neither home-made nor a product of self-service. It is given. And in this givenness and our reaction to it our existence is confirmed as being true or false. It is thus the question of truth which arises as central in the context of faith, and it arises as the question how far our existence is true. " The ground of religion lies in our whole existence and outside the sphere of our powers of knowing, which taken all together constitute the most casual and most abstract mode of our existence."[2]

Towards the end of his life, in a letter to Jacobi of 29 April, 1787, we find the most thoroughgoing relativism ascribed not only to reason, but also to human life and faith, and it is here that we find the true proportions of the whole vexed controversy as they appear to Hamann:

Being, faith, reason are sheer relationships, which do not permit themselves to be treated as absolutes. They are not things, but pure concepts of the schools, signs for the understanding and not for admiration, helps to awaken and fix our attention, just as nature is a revelation not of itself but of a

[1] G 504.   [2] R IV, 328-9 = N III, 191.

higher object, not of its vanity but of *His* glory, which is not visible save to eyes illumined and furnished with weapons, and can only be made visible under new conditions, with new instruments and institutions, abstractions and constructions, which must just as much be given (not created out of the blue) as the old elements.

What is absolute, then, is neither faith nor reason, neither human life nor nature, but existence itself, which is given by God, and in the end is identical with him, who is existence.

In the attempt to unravel Hamann's views on faith and reason we have gone beyond the text of the *Socratic Memorabilia*. To its first readers there were other more immediately noticeable elements, in particular the praise of the man of genius. These readers found what they needed for their own work. It can hardly be doubted that the enthusiasm of the men of letters of the time was one-sided, and missed the total context of Hamann's remarks. For even the genius, the ideal figure of the Romantic movement, is in Hamann's eyes not just the uncommon man, to whom no rules apply. He is the individual, the exception, whom every man may become. He is the man of faith. But this much can be said, that for the men of letters as well as the theologians (though the latter have been slower to perceive it than the poets) the break with the man of the Enlightenment, the assured, calculating, harmonious construction of the abstracting reason, is clear: as clear, indeed, as the break with the man of pietism or of orthodoxy. Hamann in this work throws open the way to real existence.

From January 1759 (when he returned to his father's house) till 1767 Hamann had no settled job. Then after some tentative beginnings he obtained, chiefly with the help of Kant, a post in the Customs. After his father's death in 1766 his brother continued to live with him till he died in 1778. During the time of his father's illness he entered upon his unofficial marriage, a marriage of conscience as he calls it, with Anna Regina Schumacher. As Hamann himself said, this kind of alliance was more possible in Prussia than anywhere else. I might add, except possibly in Scotland, where till very recently marriage by consent, as it is called, could be recognised in law as a properly binding personal decision. So far as Hamann was concerned this marriage lasted all his life and was a happy one. Why did he not go through with a legal ceremony? Such grounds as have been adduced from the outside do not seem to me to go as deep as the comment of the Danish scholar, Tage Schack, who says that in this marriage we see a man " on the boundary between faith and self-assertion."[1] That is to say, Hamann is expressing in his marriage the immense weight which he gives to faith as the ground of his whole existence. The decision whether his marriage is really the pure expression of faith, or is an arbitrary and anti-social gesture, depends on our decision about the reality of his whole life as a life of faith. Certainly, Hamann himself speaks of the arrangement as being aimed at not " lessening her happiness," and adds:

> This ongoing romance of my life, which has now been running for seventeen years . . . is for me a true sign and miracle of the ineffable and incomprehensible plan of a higher, invisible hand . . .[2]

Kierkegaard, whose whole authorship arises on the ruins of his engagement with his Regina, knew only some years after the decisive events of Hamann's marriage of conscience; but he was honest enough to see that this knowledge would probably not have made any real difference to his own decision. At a still later date he wrote in his diary, " If I had had faith I should have married Regina." Here too the resemblance, and the clear

[1]Op. cit. 239.   [2] R V, 193, a letter to Herder, 14 October, 1776.

difference, between the fates of the two men, are a striking commentary on their whole view of the meaning of existing in faith.

Just as in London, when he discovered the depth of a real existence in faith, Hamann made what from the world's standpoint can only be called the naïve and foolish remark that God would pay his debts (£300 in all), so now in this matter of his marriage he likewise turned direct to God. In 1763, that is, in the midst of this whole problem, he wrote to J. G. Lindner in Riga:

> One must give oneself with just as much confidence to the stream of circumstances as to the stream of the passions when God is with us and our life is hidden in him . . . If you see your friend on the list of tax-gatherers [a reference to the possible post at the excise office], do not be annoyed . . . I will remain on the farthest shore, or begin to serve from below, as low as ever I can.[1]

" To serve from below " is true not only of his relation to the world in his marriage, but also in his job, in his authorship, and in the whole course of his life. Without exaggeration his life may be summed up as bearing the form of a servant, in strict allusion to Christ whose life was humiliation, and in whose life Hamann found God's speech to himself. So towards the end of the first year after his homecoming he could write, " I recognise with gratitude and humility that God has driven me into a field full of thistles and thorns."[2] And in his letter applying for a job in the Royal Prussian Office of War and Property, 1 August, 1763 (a job which he got, but resigned after a few months), he writes in the following strain of stern and proud humility— but the humility is the chief element:

[1] R III, 185 = B II, 192 (cf. B II, 186: " to start serving from the bottom, even in love, makes good warriors.").
[2] R I, 493 = B I, 428.

Since I have studied simply to while away the time, and in order to humble myself, I must renounce all offices for which the quality of a *literatus* is required, and can neither refer to any merits, nor bind myself to any conditions, other than that I can if need be write legibly and do a little arithmetic ...[1]

It may therefore without exaggeration be said that Hamann's life, so impractical, so full of debts and worries, *mala* as well as *gaudia domestica*—in a word, his foolish life—is touched with the serenity of one who is a fool for Christ's sake.

[1] B II, 224.

4

THE WORD

I HAVE spoken of Hamann's humility, and derived it from his lively sense of God's condescension to the world in Christ. This derivation dominates his whole thinking. In particular, it lies behind his conception of language and his æsthetic ideas in general; and it dominates his approach to nature and history as well as to reason.

In Nadler's words, Hamann was " thoroughly penetrated by the Logos."[1] Everything was for Hamann a sign or symbol of the divine. But when Hamann makes use of the words of Hippocrates, πάντα θεῖα καὶ ἀνθρώπινα πάντα[2] to express this sense of the interpenetration of the human with the divine, he is by no means suggesting a restoration of some alleged primeval unity of the divine and the human, of religion and culture. But he is strictly bound by the conception of the Word which he finds given through the Bible in Christ.

This means that the simultaneous reference to the divine and the human which he perceives in the Logos is always a *communicatio*, never a *unio*. The Logos has for Hamann not a mythological but an eschatological significance. It is the failure to perceive this which makes Unger's whole analysis of Hamann, in his pioneer work, *Hamann und die Aufklärung*, fall short of the truth. It is worth giving a typical extract from Unger's work:

Not subordination of religion to culture, or culture to religion,

[1] J. Nadler, *Johann Georg Hamann*, Vienna, 1949, 218 (" vom Logos so völlig durchdrungen ").
[2] R II, 95 = N II, 105: cf. R IV, 23 = N III, 27.

still less the sucking up of one into the other, not simple divorce or indifferent juxtaposition, but restoration of the original unity on a higher plane, organic synthesis! In this movement towards the restoration of the original synthesis of religion and culture, of the divine and the human, the Magus, for whom the mystery of " anthropomorphosis " and " apotheosis " represented the " world-knot " (to speak with Schopenhauer), and was incarnate in the " Logos," the world symbol in large, and in God-given human language in little, sought also the solution of the basic questions of philosophy and epistemology, of history, language and æsthetics . . . not the question of an either-or . . . but of a Christianity grasped almost in the sense of the original monism of mythological prehistorical times . . .[1]

Metzke, on the other hand, justly speaks of the words of Hippocrates as meaning for Hamann " not a mystical interpenetration but a paradoxical unity."[2] It is the central Christian paradox, the Word made flesh, that is, forgiving and restoring man, which guides Hamann's thinking, and not the movement towards any alleged pre-historical or mythological monism.

What does this mean for Hamann's understanding of the relation of religion and culture? Emmanuel Hirsch, in his masterly survey of modern theological thought, understands very well the importance for Hamann of the place of faith in his whole view of life. But he maintains that this is bound to lead to a position in which no cultural life is possible. " Hamann's standpoint, if followed out logically, denies the possibility of a cultural life determined by Christianity."[3] Certainly Unger's view of a primitive organic unity of religion and culture in Hamann's life cannot be maintained. But Hirsch too has failed to perceive the dialectical nature of Hamann's faith. The tension of contradic-

[1] I, 193. [2] Op. cit., 171. [3] Op. cit., IV, 181.

tions in Hamann's view of faith is not abolished either by a pietist dualism or a mythological monism. But the tension is continually overcome in the existence of the believer. This existence of the believer is a response to a whole revelation, in the senses, in nature and in history, and it is precisely because of this wholeness and orderliness of all things in the hands of God that a faith arises which does not negate and destroy, but builds up, what is given in this way by God. For Hamann, therefore, true culture is only possible in virtue of the Word.

How may we define more particularly his conception of the Word? First, quite simply, we find it expressed in a letter to Jacobi of 22 January, 1785,[1] where he speaks of " God's inexpressible love in the Son of love " as " the centre and sun of our system." This is a clear echo of his London experience, when, for example, he writes in his *Biblical Reflections*:

> How God the Son lowered himself! He became a man, the least among men; he took the form of a servant; he became the most wretched among men; he became sin for us. How God the Holy Spirit lowered himself, when he became a historian of the smallest, most despised and insignificant events on earth, in order to reveal the decisions, the mysteries and the ways of the godhead to man in man's own language, man's own affairs, man's own ways.[2]

This condescension of love is not, however, a mere *tour de force*, to attract our attention or engage our admiration. But it is the necessary mode of God's speech with us. So again, we read:

> Scripture cannot speak with us men except in parables, since all our knowledge comes through the senses and through figures . . .[3]

The thought becomes more complex, but still derives from

[1] G 55.   [2] R I, 85-6 = N I, 91.   [3] R I, 99 = N I, 157-8.

the same source in God's Word in Christ, in a remarkable letter which Hamann wrote to Lindner shortly after he had returned to Königsberg from London:

> The invisible nature of our soul is revealed by means of words—as creation is a speech whose line stretches from one end of heaven to the other. Only the Spirit of God could tell us the miracles of the six days in so profound and comprehensible a manner. Between an idea in our soul and a sound produced by the lips lies the distance between spirit and body, heaven and earth. Yet what inconceivable bond unites these two things which are so distant from one another? Is it not a humbling of our thoughts that they cannot, so to speak, become visible except in the crude clothing of arbitrary signs? And what a proof of divine omnipotence—and humility—that he was both willing and able to breathe into the babbling and confused tongues of human ideas, with their servant's form, the depths of his mysteries and the treasures of his wisdom. Thus as a man ascends the throne of heaven, there to rule, so human language is the royal language in the praised fatherland of the Christian. How blessed we are! For he created us after his image, and because we lost it he took on our image, flesh and blood, and like a child learned to weep, to stammer, to talk, to read, to speak like a true son of man. He imitated us, that he might encourage us to imitate him.[1]

It is thus characteristic of Hamann that his thought about language, about nature and history, indeed about all human experience, is controlled by his faith in the Word made flesh. The central thought is a strictly theological one—that of the anthropomorphosis of Christ and the apotheosis of man, which is at the same time the twofold movement and mystery in every believer's life:

[1] 9 (?3) August, 1759, R I, 449-50 = B I, 393-4.

This mustard-seed of anthropomorphosis and apotheosis which is hidden in the heart and mouth of every religion, appears here [i.e., in Christ] in the form of a tree of knowledge and of life in the midst of the garden—all philosophical contradictions, and the whole historical riddle of our existence, the impenetrable night of its *terminus a quo* and its *terminus ad quem*, are resolved by the primal message of the Word become flesh.[1]

The resolution, then, of the riddle of existence, and with it of philosophical contradictions, that dizziness of reason before the enigma of its own limits, is found by Hamann in this faith in the Word made flesh. This is an eschatological faith, and an eschatological solution. That is to say, the faith really is a faith, and not a vision or sight of the resolution of the enigma. It is faith in this Word of God, and this Word is not a state or condition which can be acquired or possessed, but it is a relation. This eschatological Word is something that happens to him; it is " a living speech directed to him in each moment."[2]

This does not mean a realised eschatology in the fashionable modern sense, which tends as it were to elide the consummation of the end with history, especially with the redemptive events of Israel's history and Christ's life; or, more precisely, tends to assimilate the thought of the end to a notion of God's purpose as working itself out completely within ongoing history, i.e. in an immanent way. For if you over-stress the realisation of the end of history in certain historical events in too undialectical a manner, you tend to lose the force of God's transcendent purpose in a series of tied events which are then easily capable of an immanental and entirely human explanation. A more balanced eschatology combines the realisation of God's purpose in certain past historical events with their thoroughly proleptic nature. This is Hamann's understanding of the Word, and it means that

[1] R IV, 330 = N III, 192.   [2] Schack, op. cit., 192.

he can discern a concentration in and through *all* events of nature, history, art and language, of God's transcendent purpose. All events may therefore be signs which are transparent to God's being: they point to him, and in doing so they establish a relation with him; which involves action, something done to men. Thus in his first letter to the Swiss pastor, Lavater, Hamann writes:

> To express my soul to you from the depths, my whole Christianity . . . is a taste for *signs* and for the elements of water, bread, wine. Here is fullness for hunger and thirst—a fullness which unlike the Law is not just a shadow of future goods, but αὐτὴν τὴν εἰκόνα τῶν πραγμάτων, in so far as, through a glass darkly, it can be made present and visible; for the τελειον lies beyond (in the transcendent).[1]

This "taste for signs," then, comes from Hamann's controlling experience of God's Word speaking to him through the Bible, and it has its natural outcome in the strict sacramentalism of orthodox Christian practice. But at the same time it reaches into all experience. So he can also say, "every book is a Bible for me,"[2] by which he means, as I understand it, that the Bible is for him the clue to all other speech. Here, in the Bible, the highest things can only be expressed by the lowest means, heaven by means of earth, spirit by means of body, God by means of man. And it is not otherwise with all other human experience, and all other books. So language is the clue to Hamann's view of existence. It is the presupposition for all intellectual apprehension. But language is always a sign, and therefore not in the least a means of disclosing man's soul. It is a sign, a bridge thrown across the gulf between itself and truth. So there is no naked or direct truth, but truth comes to us as a relation, clothed in words,

---

[1] R V, 278, 17 January, 1778.
[2] B I, 309, a letter of 21 March, 1759 to Lindner. The context is: "Bible reading and prayer are a Christian's work, as novels and the dressing-table are the dandy's. Every book is a Bible for me, and every occupation a prayer."

in images which can become signs for us. So at its fullest language is a communication of existence, of the existing truth, of the Word behind the words. So all human speech points beyond itself, and tends towards its own abolition, to the point where everything ends, where we do not know but are known (I Corinthians, 13. 12).

If we look at the line of thought in Hamann's specifically æsthetic work, the *Æsthetica in Nuce* (published in 1762 as the chief piece in a collection of essays entitled *Kreuzzüge eines Philologen*—" Crusades of a Philologian "), we find that this eschatological thought about the Word dominates what he has to say. The second paragraph of the work contains words which were to be of explosive power for the *Sturm und Drang*:

Poetry is the mother-tongue of the human race, as the garden is older than the field, painting than writing, song than declamation, parables than inferences, barter than commerce. The rest of our earliest forebears was a deeper sleep; and their movement was a tumultuous dance. Seven days they sat in the silence of reflection or astonishment; and opened their mouths to utter winged words. Senses and passions speak and understand nothing but images. The whole treasure of human knowledge and happiness consists of nothing but images. The first outburst of creation, and the first impression of its historian, the first appearance and the first enjoyment of nature, are united in the words, Let there be light. Herewith begins the experience of the presence of things.[1]

But the concluding sentences of the work run as follows:

Fear God and give him the honour, for the time of his judgment is come, and pray to him who has made heaven and earth and sea and wells of water![2]

[1] R II, 258-9 = N II, 197; cf. 195ff., below. [2] R II, 308 = N II, 217.

70

It is this ending, which points to God's coming, to the *eschaton* or end, which dominates the whole argument of the work. That is to say, art, poetry, painting and music, rest upon the senses and passions. These are given to man, who is God's masterpiece, created in God's image. The whole world of creation is likewise God's world. Everything that is, is a sign of him, an image of him which we grasp through our " experience of the presence of things." " ' Speak that I may see thee!' This wish was fulfilled in the creation, which is a speaking to the creature through the creature."[1]

Speech is translation—from the language of angels into the language of men, that is, thoughts into words, things into names, images into signs, which can be poetical or literal, historical or hieroglyphical, philosophical or characteristic . . .[2]

Poetry is an imitation of nature, and man's creative power in art is an analogy of God's creative act. So nature and art point direct to God. This is the basic eschatological thought which introduces Hamann's call for freedom in the arts, for liberation from pettifogging restrictions. For art, like man himself, is unpredictable, and full of contradictions. As every man is meant to be an original and not a copy,[3] so art must be free from laws and rules, from the abstractions and conceptions of the philosophers. So the wonders of nature, works of art, and Christian life, are interlocked: they are all alike given by God as signs of his creative freedom.

This very brief survey of the *Æsthetica in Nuce* indicates its freshness and force as a literary manifesto. It certainly did work as a ferment in the poets and men of letters of the time. But it did so as it were *en passant*, as a result of Hamann's reception of God's Word into his existence as a whole rather than into his

[1] R II, 261 = N II, 198.   [2] R II, 262 = N II, 199.
[3] Cf. R II, 197 = N II, 163 (in *Chimärische Einfälle*, a defence of Rousseau against icisms of Moses Mendelssohn).

71

specialised theories about art. We have here an example of the way in which fundamental Christian experience, more powerful than any dogmatic constructions concerning it, can illuminate and even transform whole areas of human experience. Therefore it is for Hamann a consequence that the whole deposit of human experience, in culture and society, and especially in works of art, is not to be understood either by a reference back to some mythological age of religion and culture, or by a reference to external norms and principles of taste and reason, which is really no more than a kind of veiled subjectivism. But he sees the significance of art—as of nature and of man—in its immersion in the sense world which is at the same time a sign world, pointing to the hope of renewal. This hope rests upon the Word which makes all things new: it is a happening as well as a declaration. The Word is the union of the spirit with the concrete. So the whole meaning of the world consists in its being God's Word. That is, in and through the world, in the signs given in the happenings and constructions of the world, we receive a message, a word, not a law or a chain of reasoning, but a word " in and through the presence of things."

So we may see how a life based on Christian freedom, freedom in the Spirit, is immersed in the life of the senses and passions, yet not in their thrall, not absorbed, but seeing in and through this world that which holds everything together—not an eternal Idea, not a great Mathematician, not an inference from a discursive argument, but the Word which is relation with God, man's and the world's only relation with God: this is an eschatological faith in which the whole of creation may be renewed. In Hamann's words, as he describes the original state of creation, which is for him a symbol of the hope which animates him:

So Adam was God's; and God himself introduced the first-born and oldest of our race as the bearer and heir of the world which had been made ready by the word of his mouth. Angels, happy to look upon his heavenly countenance, were the ministers and courtiers of the first monarch. All the children of God were jubilant to the choir of the morning stars. At first hand, from the pristine act, all of them tasted and saw the friendliness of the Maker, who played on his earth and had joy in his human children. As yet no creature had been cast against its will into the vanity and bondage of the transient system under which they now yawn and sigh . . . Every phenomenon of nature was a word, the sign, image and pledge of a new, mysterious, inexpressible, but for that reason all the more inward union, communication and community of divine energies and ideas. Everything that man in the beginning heard, saw, gazed upon, and touched, was a living word. For God was the Word. With this Word in his mouth and in his heart the origin of language was as natural, as near and easy, as a child's game. For human nature is from the beginning to the end of days just as like to the kingdom of heaven as to a tiny bit of yeast with which every woman can ferment three measures-ful of flour.[1]

From this faith flow two corollaries in particular, which agitated Hamann all his life. The first is his view of the origin of language, which involved him in controversy with his old friend and disciple, Herder. The second is his view of the relation of language to the senses and to experience, on the one hand, and to the function of reason, on the other hand, in which his chief antagonist was Kant.

Before we look at these two matters, it might be helpful to draw out the implications of Hamann's view of the Word in relation to conventional theological symbols.

First, we must ask whether Hamann's conception of the Word

[1] R IV, 32-4 = N III, 32.

may fairly be identified with the orthodox view of the Word. The answer can only be, Yes and No: with the intention of orthodoxy, Yes, with its customary restriction, No.

The intention of the orthodox doctrine of the Word is, first, to establish the reality of this world, of the whole cosmos, as God's creation, the utterance of his Word, that is, his particular will conjoined with his complete fulfilment of that will. God's Word in creation is therefore the fullness of his being in action. There is no reservation of God in his Word: what he says he does, and what he does is entirely and fully his being. His being is therefore his action in his Word. Therefore the cosmos is neither a mere appearance, nor is it a reduction of God's being. This is the first meaning of the Word as identical with God.

The second intention of the orthodox doctrine of the Word of God is to express in similar contingent form the real identity of God's will and action in the historical person of Christ. This contingent Word is again neither mere appearance nor a reduction of God. The accommodation of God to man's life does not take place by means of an emptying of the reality of God's being. The modern theories of the *kenosis* or self-emptying of God (derived from the Pauline reference in Philippians, 2. 7ff.) contain, indeed, a remarkable appeal to man's pity, to his sense of the tragedy of existence; but they are able to do this only by yielding up the reality of the fullness of God's presence in his Word in Christ.

Now Hamann recognises, with greater clarity than any other writer since the time of Luther, the humbleness of God's word to man. He speaks of " the whole of creation " as " a work of the greatest humility," of the " son of God in his servant's form " as being a " lowering " of God and an " emptying of his majesty."[1] He speaks frequently of the Bible as being altogether like the rags and worn-out clothes which the Ethiopian used to

[1] R II, 207 == N II, 171.

74

help Jeremiah up out of the cistern into which he had been cast (Jeremiah, 38. 7ff.).[1]

But this lowliness is the reality of God. This necessary mode of God's speech with man is at the same time the reflection of what God really is, namely, one who gives himself in humble and powerless love to his world. Certainly, God is veiled or concealed in this lowliness, and as Hamann says, this is to offend the wise and the clever, but also to lead men through this same humility, through " the poverty of a book," through the folly of Christ's life, to discern God's presence:

> If therefore the divine style chooses the foolish, the shallow, the ignoble, to put to shame the strength and ingenuity of all profane writers, there certainly is need of the illuminated, enthused and eager eyes of a friend, an intimate, a lover, in order to discern through such a disguise the beams of heavenly glory. *Dei dialectus soloecismus* [" God speaks bad grammar "].[2]

None of this implies a restriction of the Word to any static form, whether of the written Word of the Bible, or of the dim figure of the historical Jesus. The Word of God is never for Hamann an assemblage of propositions or truths of doctrine demanding our assent. The Word of God as God's way of relation with man, and man's with God, is not confined. The truth is the Spirit, and the Spirit is not bound. There is in this understanding of the Word a dynamic conception of God's action, in creation, in redemption, and in history in the most comprehensive sense. In the following section I shall have more to say about Hamann's view of history. In the meantime I anticipate only to say that for him history is no more and no less important than nature as a commentary on the Word given in

---

[1] The image occurs four times in all, in N J, 176; B I, 341; R V, 281; G 38.
[2] R II, 207-8 = N II, 171.

Scripture. The whole conception is of the Word of God as theonomous, as active, as present, and as spilling over the conventional static forms in which orthodoxy often attempts to restrict this Word. For Hamann every happening, every speech of the creature with the creature, every situation or event, every human enterprise in art or language, may be the Word of God. There is an absence of separation here, a wholeness of his view of the world, which Goethe was quick to discern, when he spoke in *Dichtung und Wahrheit* of Hamann's one principle, that " everything man undertakes, whether produced in act or word or otherwise, must spring from total united powers; everything separated is to be repudiated."[1] Goethe recognised the result in Hamann's writing; but he did not acknowledge the cause; or if he did, he shunned it—as indeed he shunned any direct communication with Hamann.

Hamann's understanding of revelation, second, is likewise expansive and generous. He makes no distinction between the natural and the supernatural. " All natural knowledge is revealed," he writes in the *Biblical Reflections* as early as 1758, and nothing in his later views alters that fundamental and far-reaching unity.[2] But this is by no means a merely romantic, far less a pantheistic commingling of spheres. Hamann means that every thing we have, every experience, every encounter, in nature or in history, comes from outside us. It is given to us. Alike in faith and in reason we do not make anything, we simply receive. " To receive, more emptiness than strength is required, more repose than participation," he wrote to Jacobi.[3] This is not the assertion of a mystical self-emptying, the preparation for absorption in the godhead. Hamann is at every point of his life poles apart from the mystics, whether those within or those outside the traditional Christian scheme. But Hamann means here, as in so many places, that all our experience is really revelation. " Ex-

[1] Ch. 12. [2] R I, 115 = N I, 222. [3] Letter of 23 January, 1785.

perience and revelation are one and the same," he writes to
Jacobi.[1] They are the foundation of all human knowledge.
So the correlate of faith is revelation:

> So we see that in our faith alone are heavenly knowledge, true
> happiness and the loftiest freedom of our human nature united.
> Doctrines of Reason, of spirit and of morals are three daughters
> of a true doctrine of nature, which has no better source than
> revelation.[2]

Revelation therefore runs through the whole of creation,
through nature and history and the life of man, as it were a secret
treasure waiting to be disclosed to the attendant faith.

This view of revelation, like his view of the Word, goes far
beyond the customary divisions, whether of revealed and natural
knowledge in the standard Roman Catholic view, or of general
and particular revelation in modern Protestant writing. For
Hamann everything can be revelation, and this revelation is
always of the one Word. Metzke rightly notes[3] that for Hamann
there is "in principle no limitation of revelation." We might
add, there is no limitation of the Word. The whole world is a
speech or conversation with God.

> The products of human art, science and history all serve as the
> seal, the human seal, of revelation, and one has as a Christian
> as little reason to dispense with them or abolish them as Paul
> had to abandon his cloak in Troas.[4] (And later he writes):
> In the histories, laws and customs of all nations we find what
> we may term the *sensum communem* of religion. Everything
> lives and is full of hints of our calling and of the God of grace.
> We are very prejudiced if we limit God's effects and influence
> merely to the Jewish people. In the example of that people

---

[1] 14 November, 1784.   [2] R I, 136 = N I, 302.   [3] Op. cit., 150, n. 2.
[4] R I, 119 = N I, 241.

he has merely declared and made available to our senses the hiddenness, the method and the laws of his wisdom and love; and has left to us the application of this to our own life and to other objects, peoples and events.[1]

In these two quotations it may be seen how Hamann, by immensely enlarging, has tacitly abandoned the views of revelation to be found in orthodoxy, pietism and rationalism.

He is hospitable also to the qualities and significance of other religions than the Christian, for here too experience is one with revelation. Thus he writes:

One can perhaps not deny to all other nations the analogy of a similar dim inkling and perception [to that of the Jewish nation] . . .[2]

Similarly, he speaks of nature as being also revelation, but at once adds, " but not a revelation of itself, but of a higher object, not of its own unity but of his glory."[3] But even when he speaks of nature and history as the two great revelations of God—" as nature is given to us to open our eyes, so history is given to us to open our ears "[4]—he always means that this giving is dependent upon God's gift, and specifically upon his gift in the Bible. " Nature and history are the two great commentaries on the divine Word [i.e. the Bible], and this Word is the only key to unlock a knowledge of both."[5]

So we are continually brought back to the Word which is given in the history of the Jewish people. And the facts of this history, like the facts given in nature, our sense-experience, are all available to us as revelation waiting upon faith. " Facts rest upon faith," he says,[6] and this is not a diminution of the significance of the senses, but on the contrary tends towards

[1] R I, 136-7 = N I, 303.   [2] R VII, 56 = N III, 311.   [3] G 513.   [4] R II, 17 = N II, 64.   [5] R I, 138 = N I, 303.   [6] G 668.

an unprecedented exaltation of the senses as the source of all knowledge, that is, as the place of revelation.

For in the end revelation for Hamann is simply all that is: it is the only proper knowledge, as it is the only proper understanding of all human experience:

> [Everything] the treasure-house of faith as well as the warehouse of reason, rests ... upon our five senses which we have in common with the brute creation.[1] Nothing is in our understanding which was not previously in our senses.[2]

In sum, then, we can say that for Hamann revelation comes through the senses, it is grounded upon sense-experience, and it is a Word to the whole of human existence. Human existence is what it can be only when it is turned out from itself into the whole action of God in his creation. Man's life is therefore to be seen as a reaction to God's action, a response to his Word. It is as participants in a conversation with God, in and through conversation with the whole of creation, that men come to God, and so, incidentally, come to themselves.

With such views it is clear that in the controversy of his time about the origin of language Hamann was bound to maintain its divine origin—yet in no crass manner. I have already quoted a famous passage in which Hamann describes in rhapsodic language the state of Adam in relation to the rest of creation and to God. There we can see how for Hamann the whole reality of man's existence consists in his receptivity, his *Empfänglichkeit*, his reaction to the given experiences which are the gift of God. Out of this situation speech arose as easily and naturally as child's play. But it is always God's gift and not man's effort which counts. Hamann would certainly not discount the psychological and the traditional factors which make for the growth and characteristic

[1] R I, 127 = N I, 298. [2] R IV, 44 = N III, 39.

particularities of various languages. In fact, he showed great interest in the structure of languages, and was one of the first philologists to draw attention to the setting and even the history of a people as portrayed in their language. His remarks on the nature of New Testament Greek, for instance, showed an insight into the nature of the *koiné* which was far ahead of his time.[1]

But in the setting of the discussion Hamann's view was clear. The controversy was fundamentally a reflection of the more general theme which occupied so much attention in the eighteenth century, the theme, namely, of the relation of faith and reason, of natural and revealed religion, of the supernatural and the natural. Briefly, there were three possible standpoints: (1) that language was established by arbitrary agreement. This is the Aristotelian position, as maintained by John Locke, for instance, in his *Essay concerning Human Understanding*, III, and widely accepted throughout the period of the Enlightenment. (2) A more naturalistic theory, developed by Hobbes, also found its supporters, notably Condillac in his *Essai sur l'origine des connoissances humaines* (1746-54). This view differed from the first only in attempting to explain how language gradually arose out of the social instincts and needs of men. (3) Directly opposed to all such rationalising views is the stiffly orthodox Christian view as represented in crassest style by Bishop William Warburton, in his *The Divine Legation of Moses* (1738-41). According to this view, a direct and miraculous intervention of God is the origin of human language.[2]

Is it possible to rescue, as it were, the ground and space for supernatural explanations, for miracle and divine intervention, in this matter of the origin of language? As the controversy was established, with its hidden presuppositions about the validity or

---

[1] Cf. R II, 201-212 = N II, 167-173; also 186f below (*e.g.*, " What an author intends, where and when he lives, are all determinative of the way he expresses himself.").

[2] A fuller survey of the controversy will be found in R. Unger, *Hamanns Sprachtheorie*, Munich, 1905, 155ff.

non-validity of the function and place of revelation, it seems
inevitable that a more or less rationalist and naturalistic explanation
had to be sought. This was the view of Herder, Hamann's friend
and disciple. In his prize essay on the *Origin of Language*, published
in 1772, he develops his view in terms of a sharp distinction of
man from the animals. Man possesses, in distinction from the
animals, a wide and manifold power, and his senses and instincts
are superior to those of the animals in virtue of his possession of
freedom. Man's whole life is guided by a conscious and purpo-
sive power which at once unifies, expands and liberates his bodily
and spiritual powers. This particular and distinctive power
Herder calls *Besonnenheit*, a power of concentration, of reflection,
which includes both the reasoning and the instinctive powers in
man. Out of this power, which is peculiar to man, human speech
is discovered.

For Hamann these views meant a betrayal of his dearest beliefs.
For him language was the expression of man's utter dependence
upon God. Man is born with nothing. He can do nothing by
himself. He has to be taught everything. He has nothing innate
at all. Everything we have is from God. We accept, we learn,
we receive, and in all this we are not different from the rest of the
animals, but stand alongside them as God's creatures. Hamann's
interest, it must be admitted, did not lie in any psychological
investigations into human nature, far less in any concern for
man's inborn dignity. But he was concerned with the nature of
man, which for him meant only one thing: man's relation to
God.

Herder himself expostulated with Hamann in a letter in which
he said, in effect, that his essay did not deal with the divine origin
of man (and thus of language). " That God effected language
through, by means of, men," was not what he was discussing,
and this, like Hamann, he did not doubt.[1] Perhaps Herder was

---

[1] Cf. letter to Hamann of 1 August, 1772, R V, 7ff.

somewhat disingenuous when faced with his angry and dis-
illusioned mentor. At any rate, Hamann clung to his position.
Man's nature over against God is not characterised by harmony,
dignity, reasonableness and power—whether *Besonnenheit* or anything else—but by the word of the Psalmist, " I am a worm and
no man," by a sense of his nothingness, and of God's being everything. Hamann's case rests, therefore, not upon mythological
inspirations nor upon psychological investigations, but upon a
stark anthropology. The reality of man's life depends utterly upon
God, upon man's response to God's Word to him.

It may be said that Hamann short-circuits the discussion, and
that he is standing for just as incomprehensible a position as
Bishop Warburton. But I think that he stands for more: for the
lively recognition of the ultimate inconclusiveness and un-
satisfactory nature of any discussion which starts from the presupposition of a clean break between what man is by himself,
and what God is. Man by himself is an abstraction, it is man
with God who is truly human. So Hamann lives by faith.
But at the same time it is not a faith which merely ignores the
natural life of man. " All things are divine, and they are also
human," is a thought which is often in his mind.[1] And in one
of his retorts to Herder, *Des Ritters von Rosenkreuz letzte Willens-
meinung über den göttlichen und menschlichen Ursprung der Sprache*
(" The Knight of Rosenkreuz's Last Will about the divine and
human origin of language "), he speaks quite plainly not only of
a divine origin, but also a human origin; quoting with approval
the words of Protagoras, that " man is the measure of all things."[2]
He can do this because it is precisely in and through the natural
life of man that he recognises man's utter dependence upon the
world outside him; and this world is God's Word: it is not a
separate or autonomous entity in which man does things for and
by himself, whether it is the invention of language or the dis-

[1] R II, 95 = N II, 105.   [2] R IV, 23 = N III, 27; and see 247, below.

covery of God. To speak of a "natural language," just as to speak of "natural religion," is for Hamann a complete mis-interpretation of man's life, it is an *Unding*, a non-thing, an *ens rationis*. As he says in a letter to Herder of 26 June, 1780 (that is, long after the immediate controversy and strain between the two had died down):

> First, natural religion is for me, like a natural language, a veritable *Unding*, an *ens rationis*. Second, what is called natural religion is just as problematic and polemic as revelation. And why the readiness to chew over and refine that which the true *ton de siècle sub umbra alarum* is? Reason is Moses in person, and our modern philosophy is the Pope transfigured. Judaism, its spirit, natural religion, is the universal solution, to judge by *Jerusalem*, Büsching, etc. Scarcely a thought of the Messiah . . .[1]

This is not to say that for Hamann all revelation is reduced to the level of the simply natural; but rather the other way round, that all nature is the vehicle of revelation. There cannot be a natural religion because all religion is revelation, religion through nature equally with religion through Scripture and history. So far as language is concerned, therefore, it, like everything else, can only be understood in terms of the relation between God and man. It is even possible to say that for Hamann God can no more be understood without man than man can be understood without God. This does not mean the loss of God's transcendence, but rather the affirmation of his continual presence through his Word. Between God and man there is a constant commerce, without loss of identity: God becoming man, man raised to God, anthropomorphosis and apotheosis.

In his lifelong controversy with Kant it is again his view of man's being as grounded in God's Word which provides the best

[1] R VI, 143.

clue to his concern. This comes out clearly in his *Metakritik über den Purismus der Vernunft* ("Metacritique of the Purism of Reason "),[1] a work as obscure in its details as almost any writing can be. Nevertheless, the main drift is clear. In allusion to Kant's *Critique of Pure Reason*, Hamann here makes the ironical suggestion that Kant has not gone far enough. He has purified the reason of experience, as his predecessors in the *Aufklärung* had purified reason of tradition and history. Now there is a third step which ought surely to be taken: the purification of reason of language itself. Language has a double root, or rather, two branches but only one root: it has the branch of what Hamann calls *Sinnlichkeit* and *Anschauung*, that is, the branch which belongs to the senses, to sense-experience, to the sounds and letters of language; and it has the branch which belongs to the understanding and to concepts, to the element of the significant. Kant should really be logical and eliminate the remnants of the sense world from language. But of course Hamann's point is that this cannot in fact be done. You cannot banish the sense world, which is still visible in language, to the realm of appearances. Not even Kant can do this, for in the heart of his so-called " pure " reason is language, which is firmly bound to the world of sense and experience. That is why Hamann can also say that Kant's " transcendental " is not really *transcendent* at all, but is " on this side of experience."[2]

It is worth recalling that Hamann knew only the first of the *Critiques*, and that it is Kant's epistemology and not his religious standpoint as a whole which he is here criticising. In the introduction to the second edition of the *Critique of Pure Reason* Kant wrote that he " found it necessary to deny knowledge in order to make room for faith," and as early as 1763 he spoke of the " bottomless abyss " of metaphysics, and compared it to a " dark ocean without

---

[1] I have attempted a translation of the whole piece, see 213ff, below.
[2] Cf. Metzke, op. cit., 165.

either shore or lighthouse."[1] This is not the language of arrogant reason, and it is possible to argue that Kant was much more on the side of the Romantics than Hamann ever recognised. Nevertheless, in the use of reason in the attempt to establish the scope of reason Hamann perceives a basic illegitimacy which he here focuses on the understanding of the nature of language. On his understanding it is not even possible to regard space and time as *a priori* intuitions, for the concept of space springs from painting, the oldest form of writing, and the concept of time springs from music, the oldest form of speech. Seeing and hearing are thus deeply embedded in space and time, Kant's so-called pure forms.

In this criticism it is possible to see something beyond the ideas of the so-called " Faith philosophers," and indeed, as Friedrich Blanke has suggested, there are hints in Hamann's views of what were later to be called the phenomenological views of a writer like Husserl about the direct givenness of things.[2]

But for Hamann himself the force of his argument leads him back on his old tracks, the strong hold on the empirical world, and the equally strong sense of its givenness from God. The " givenness of things " is in his view never purely arbitrary, but is always at the same time a sign, a speech, *the* Word. When he says, for instance, that " the whole ability to think rests upon language,"[3] that " language is the sole . . . instrument and criterion of reason,"[4] that " without language there can be no reason,"[5] and that language is the " Deipara, the mother of our reason,"[6] he is thinking all the time of what he elsewhere explicitly says:

Without the Word there is no reason, no world. Here is the source of creation and government.[7]

[1] Quoted in Hirsch, op. cit., IV, 275.
[2] Cf. F. Blanke, *Hamann-Studien*, 20-1, to whom I owe much for this attempt to understand the relations of Kant and Hamann, as well as for much more stimulus.
[3] R VII, 9 = N III, 286. [4] R VII, 6 = N III, 84. [5] R VI, 25 = N III, 231.
[6] R VI, 39 = N III, 239. [7] G 7.

So the realm of experience, of sense-experience, is at the same time the realm of revelation, and these are prior to reason:

> Experience and revelation are one and the same, and are indispensable wings or crutches for our reason, if it is not to be lame and creeping . . .[1]

No doubt Kant scholars will recognise the *naïveté* of Hamann's simple assertion that the sense world and the understanding belong together and cannot be separated. For Kant was concerned precisely with the question of *how* they belong together, and how one may make synthetic *a priori* judgments. And Kant's notion of *Einbildungskraft* or " imaginative power " indicates how near he was in his deep sympathies with the kind of position that Hamann stood for.

Nevertheless, the criticism of Kant's acceptance of language is a valid one, the significance of which is only properly becoming apparent in our time. But however much we may have to make allowances for Hamann in his view of Kant, so far as his own views are concerned he is speaking in terms which do not bear much meaning for Kant, however sympathetic Kant may have been with Hamann's general intention. For Hamann the reality of our experience lies at once in its immediacy and its mediacy: immediacy, in the sense that he cannot separate experience and understanding; mediacy, in the sense that he sees everything as given by a continuously open or possible revelation from God in his Word, and this mediate possibility is realised in faith. This does not mean that Hamann relapses into gnosticism or mysticism. On the contrary, it is Kant whom he accuses of " a gnostic hatred of the material," and of a mystical tendency to derive his transcendental apperception from his own I, i.e. from his productive reason.[2]

If I may attempt a summary of Hamann's views at this point,

[1] G 16. [2] R VI, 7 = N III, 285.

it is necessary to hold together in our minds the twofold nature of his thought about language. On the one hand he is strongly influenced by the empirical philosophers, by their grounding of all human experience in the senses, and by his determination not to be led into the subtleties of Kant's discussion. He remains a naïve sensualist, and simply does not raise Kant's question whether what we grasp by the senses is the real world or not. But on the other hand he is so deeply conscious of the nothingness of man, in a religious sense, that he carries this consciousness over without any difficulty into his understanding of the nature of human experience: it is all from outside, but more, it is all a gift. Man is a recipient, he does not make the world, he does not even make its meaning. The meaning lies in the all-pervading Word of God, so that in and through the world of the senses this Word may be discerned. So this world is an allegory or sign of the reality— not of a world of ideas, but of God as speaking and acting:

> Everything is . . . the vehicle or vestige of his influence in our flesh and blood, and of the commerce between the world above and the world below. The whole of visible nature is nothing but the face and hands of the clock; the works them- selves and the proper weight are his winds and fiery flames.[1]

In conclusion, we see in Hamann's view of language a strictly Christian apprehension of the world as the creation of God the Word, and an eschatological apprehension of the presence of the Word in man and the world. Everything is for him a symbol of the divine speech with man, but neither in a pantheist nor a mystical sense. It is not that God is everything, nor that everyone must lose himself in God. But God's Word may be heard in everything, and everyone may hear him. Not simply, of course, not direct: but in and through faith, which is always " the descent into the hell of self-knowledge."

[1] R VI, 112-3, a letter to Herder, 1 January, 1780.

5

HISTORY

HAMANN'S VIEW of history is what most distinguishes him from his own age, and at the same time brings him nearest to our time. His greatest adversary among the men of the Enlightenment—if we except Kant, who passes beyond the Enlightenment—is Lessing. Lessing too was not entirely characteristic, for in his view of the "education" of the human race, as we shall see, he did show an advance upon the normal views of the time. And he certainly thought more highly of the old religious orthodoxy than of the contemporary religious system of the Enlightenment, which he described in a letter to his brother as "a patchwork made by amateurs and half-baked philosophers."[1] But Hamann himself saw no essential change. He described *The Education of the Human Race* as "nothing but a wandering of ideas in new formulæ and words. No scheblimini, no real Reformation spirit, no conception worthy of a Magnificat."[2]

For Lessing, as for the Enlightenment generally, the key to the understanding of history may be found in the words of Leibniz:

Knowledge of eternal and necessary truths distinguishes us from the mere animals and gives us Reason and the Sciences, raising us to the knowledge of ourselves and of God.[3]

"Necessary truths of reason" were alone valid. This did not mean that Christianity was entirely ruled out. It still persisted as a power in the present by means of the teachings of Jesus. But

[1] 14 July, 1773.   [2] R VI, 139, 128.
[3] *Monadology*, § 29, in the translation of R. Latta, *The Monadology*, 1898, 233.

it did mean that historical action, with all its dialogical powers, was replaced by the monologue of the autonomous reason. And human reason, finding in historical facts no more than probabilities, abandoned " facts " in favour of " meaning," history in favour of teaching.

For Hamann it was equally true that out of history only probabilities could be reached. But the emphasis for him lay upon the fact that it was the human reason which found itself in this ambiguous position. This was the point around which Kierkegaard was later to construct the brilliant and paradoxical *Concluding Unscientific Postscript*, in which historical facts, leading only to approximations, were nevertheless the means and mode of God's self-disclosure. Though Hamann could not easily associate himself with Lessing's opponent, the orthodox Pastor Goeze, yet he could not help saying that the *Oelgoetze* or " staring idol," as he called him in a wicked pun, was " with all his stupidity " nearer right than Lessing.

Hamann was unable to drive a wedge between facts and meaning, between history and reason, as Lessing did. For it was precisely in the " facts," the events, of history that he found the point at which faith was faced with a choice and a need for decision.[1] He could not first separate the world off from reason, and then grant to reason, as a kind of free-swinging power, an autonomy and authority over against the world. This was clean contrary to his whole understanding of human experience. The powers of reason, as we have seen, were for him firmly embedded in the sense-world, and in particular in history and tradition. So to him the facts of Christian history were not in the least as Lessing saw them—as a kind of scaffolding which could be discarded once their significance had been realised. Far less could the reason of itself, without even this minimal connection with historical events, establish truths which might claim to be

[1] Cf. G 668: " Facts rest upon faith."

89

permanently and universally valid. Truths of reason in this sense simply did not exist. This is as grave a misapprehension as that of the Jews, who thought they could find in the Law the whole and sufficient way to God. Reason could only lead to an acknowledgment of ignorance, as the Law could only lead to an acknowledgment of sin:

> Reason discloses to us no more than Job saw: that our birth is unhappy, that the grave is better, that human life is unprofitable and vain; for we are without insight, and feel in ourselves passions and impulses the purpose of which we do not know.[1]

The negative pole for all Hamann's understanding is the incapacity of reason as an autonomous power to penetrate to the living truth. How then, we must ask, did Hamann understand the facts of history, especially of Christian history?

First, he recognised that they could be present. Time was the dominant factor, not as a kind of makeshift or inferior route to eternity, but as the very way of truth. That Christ came into history meant that he lived in and through time. And this controlling fact is not merely the recognition of a past event which is embalmed in the history of Palestine. But it is taken up into God's hands as a thread which gives fullness and completion to the present:

> Every moment of time is perfectly rounded; that out of each moment a line comes, is due to the thread which providence has drawn through it, and which gives it an exact connection, which our weak eyes cannot see. This thread makes the connection of moments and parts of time so firm and inseparable . . . that everything consists of one piece . . .[2]

[1] R I, 96 = N I, 147. (Cf. the remark by a modern writer, " When the intellect is faced with God it must be seized with a conviction of intellectual inadequacy parallel to the moral inadequacy with which we more commonly identify a sense of sin," M. Foster, *Mystery and Philosophy*, London, 1957, 46.)
[2] R I, 90 = N I, 125-6.

Almost thirty years later, in an abandoned first version of his last work, *A Flying Letter*, he writes even more explicitly about the significance of the present moment—and here too he points direct to Kierkegaard and through him to modern writers such as Grisebach and Martin Buber:

> What would the most exact and careful knowledge of the present be without a divine renewal of the past, without an inkling of the future? . . . What a labyrinth the present would be for the spirit of observation, without the spirit of prophecy and its clues from the past and the future![1]

This interweaving of past and future in the texture of the present means an absolute rejection of the Enlightenment distinction between eternal and temporal truths. For Hamann history lies open. There is no dead past, which can be discarded. Strictly speaking, any event of the past can live in the present. In practice, it is again and again certain luminous and numinous events of history which convey the particular transparency which is determinative for Hamann:

> The field of history has always appeared to me to be like that wide field that was full of bones, and behold they were very dry. Only a prophet can prophesy of these bones, that veins and flesh will grow on them and skin cover them. They have still no breath in them, till the prophet prophesies to the wind and the word of the Lord speaks to the wind . . .[2]

So it is the history of the Jewish people in particular which holds Hamann's attention. " All Jewish history was prophecy "—

The whole history of the Jewish people seems, in accordance with the parable of its ceremonial law, to be a living primary

[1] N III, 398.   [2] R II, 218 = N II, 176.

book, awaking spirit and heart, of all historical literature in heaven and in earth and beneath the earth . . .[1]

But if the spirit of prophecy brings clues from the past into the present, it equally speaks out of the future into the present. For this the *vis divinandi* is required, and thus Hamann writes:

Who can have right ideas of the present without knowing the future? The future determines the present, and the present determines the past, as the purpose determines the constitution and the means to be used.[2]

In this immense stress upon the present, which is rushing out of the future which is determining it, and rushing into the past over which it has likewise a renewing power, we meet the peculiarly anthropological concern which is Hamann's dominating motif. It is as an interpretation of man's being and destiny that Hamann regards history in this pregnant form. As Metzke has said, " the spatial categories of ' this world ' and ' the world beyond ' are inadequate to express the paradoxical unity of presence and transcendence " in Hamann's view.[3] This paradoxical unity might be more precisely described, in Hamann's own terminology in *A Flying Letter*, as a concentration of past and future in the present, that is, in a present determined by the future, and determining the past, which is the real end of history in God's purpose.

History on this view is not a detached structure of reasonable principles, nor a sequence of cause and effect, nor any kind of contrivance of the human reason for the explication of man's subjective impressions of the outside world. It has to do with man, but not with man in and for himself. History is therefore an interpretation of man's being and destiny in terms of a world of meaning coming from outside man. " All events of world

[1] R VII, 56 = N III, 311.   [2] R II, 217 = N II, 175.   [3] Op. cit., 229.

history," he writes, " are silhouettes of more mysterious actions and disclosed miracles."[1] But this insistence on the transcendent element in history does not destroy the historical events, or deprive them of their reality. But this reality is guaranteed and confirmed in the fact that the transcendent element is encountered in the present, that is, in man's present and contingent life.

History, then, has a double nature. On the one hand it strikes into the present life of man, demanding his free, responsible decision; and on the other hand it points to the meaning which is in God's will and power, in his freedom over against the future. But this meaning is not present as an isolated entity, capable of apprehension by the *ratio* of man. It is present as an eschatological power. That is, the end of history is present in man's personal life, and this end is God's complete action in his Word. This completeness of God's Word, that is, the completeness of his action, is what makes it possible for all historical events to be recognised as signs. But in so pointing to the " more mysterious actions " history is not abolished. There is no " eternal " or " universal " truth which is waiting to be grasped and possessed as the crown of history. But rather, in its silhouetting of transcendent actions, history, that is, man's history in its contingency and presentness, is realised in its full historicity. That is to say, history is fulfilled. To say, then, that history is a *Gleichnis*, a picture or allegory or parable, of a transcendental end, is not the destruction of the events which compose mundane history, but rather the introduction into them of a meaning greater than themselves—greater, that is, than any single event or separate chain of events, any bit of history. To speak of the " meaning of history " as a whole is strictly impossible, until we add, " as seen by God," seen, that is, at the end of history. Now the prophetic or eschatological insight which Hamann describes is precisely this view of history: it is the view from the end, the

[1] R I, 139 = N I, 304.

93

eschaton, a proleptic view, an anticipation of the end received from God in faith through revelation. History may well be called meaningless except to the man who has faith in this way. But the meaning which the man who has faith finds in history is not a meaning extraneous to itself, or added as an explanation to an otherwise hopeless enigma. The paradoxical truth is that the meaning which appears in and through the events of history, out of the transcendence of God's purpose, is at the same time these events themselves, as present to the believer, and charged with the power of God's complete purpose. History is indeed, as Hamann said,

a sealed book, a cloaked witness, a riddle which cannot be solved, unless we plough with some other ox than our reason,[1]

and here again, in opposition to the notion of universal truths permanently available to the productive and inquiring reason, he is thinking of the power of revelation in and through all events of history. It is the past as well as the future which must be revealed.[2] All history is therefore a sign of God's purpose with man and the world.

In this understanding of history, which I have based as solidly as possible on Hamann's own widely scattered and allusive remarks, it is clear that Hamann goes far beyond the customary orthodox position of his day—and, I should add, of our day. The orthodox of the time were content to accept the division of life into the two spheres of the natural and the supernatural, the sphere of the immanent and the transcendent, of knowledge and faith, of nature and grace. Their opponents, the rationalists and the naturalists, did the same. But what was not so apparent then as it is now is that this division, if accepted in a thoroughgoing way, really involves the crowding out, in the end, of the " super-

[1] R II, 19 = N II, 65. [2] R I, 90 = N I, 125.

natural " sphere from any active share in the life of man. This the rationalists, or at least some of them (Lessing certainly, and Moses Mendelssohn, the enlightened Jew) clearly perceived; and they were content, having marked out their territory, to allow the supernaturalists to cling to the crumbling battlements of their forlorn heaven with its superannuated deity.

Hamann perceived the danger, or at least he recognised the folly, of accepting this accustomed staking-out of the claims upon man. In some respects he was very ready—I should say, only too ready—to fight the rationalists on their own ground, and on their terms—hence his ceaseless belabouring of the top-heavy claims of the autonomous reason, which has led to too easy a classification of him as a mere anti-rationalist. But in all this he was at least groping towards a new conception, which admitted of a possible new ground of unity. This new ground is what I have called the eschatological standpoint, a grasp of the unity of God's purpose with the present personal life of man. This does not necessarily involve the belief in a supernatural irruption into an otherwise complete universe, conceived along deistic lines, or into a developing historical entity, conceived along naturalistic lines. But he regarded the whole of history, as we have seen, as at once the place and the manifestation of revelation. It is in this sense that all history was miraculous to him. For at every point God's Word could be heard. As early as his time in London he could write

My health and my life are at once a miracle and a sign that God did not despair of my recovery,[1]

and though this remark, and its context, have a flavour which might seem to throw him back into the camp of the pietists, in the sequel it leads to a different conception of miracle and of history than that held by either the pietists or the traditionalists.

[1] R I, 216 = N II, 42. Cf. R I, 68 = N I, 24: " What is there in nature, in the commonest and most natural events, that is not a miracle for us, a miracle in the strictest sense ? "

Miracle is not reduced to a subjective state in the soul of the believer, nor is it extracted as a weapon to supply direct historical evidence for the truth of Christianity. The miracle which Hamann sees continuing in his own life is the same miracle which he sees in all history: it is an affirmation of God's seriousness with regard to his creation. But this manifestation of God which he discerns in history is not simple and immediate: it is highly paradoxical and indirect. It is concealed at the same time as it is made manifest. It is a God incognito, a God humble and poor, who makes himself known in the events of history, in the event of Christ, and in the sacraments. So he can say that it is in the elements of water, bread and wine that he perceives the presence of the *teleion*, the end, and a *communicatio idiomatum*, as in the life of Christ himself.[1]

It is clear that on such a view historical events must remain in the centre of the picture. To say that they remain as " signs " does not mean that they are emptied of their historicity, but that they are filled with the fullness possible to them. So Hamann can even say that all monarchs

are silhouettes of the golden age where there will be one shepherd and one flock.[2]

It is just because his thought is controlled by his eschatological faith that he can discern meaning in all ongoing events. To any other view history is " a sealed book." And the biblical history in particular, with its primitive and crude stories and language, is incomprehensible on any other view. This history can of course be smoothed out and explained, as Lessing and Mendelssohn did, in terms of a theory of development. The stories are but the product of an earlier and uneducated age. But for Hamann it is precisely the crudities and contradictions and tensions which bear

[1] Cf. R VI, 6 = N III, 218, and R VI, 170 (letter to Herder, 18 December, 1770).
[2] G 642-3.

witness to the riddle of history as being at the same time the theatre of God's action and the place of his appearing. For only in such a situation is concealment possible, and therefore only in such a situation can a sign be discerned, a sign which carries in it the possibility both of offence and of faith.

If we return to the views of Lessing, in particular in *The Education of the Human Race*, we find that Lessing did represent an advance upon the old rationalism, to this extent, at least, that he was prepared to ascribe to reason a progressive life, a growth within the unfolding life of man, which is a significant concession to the place of history and historical events in the life of man. But Hamann, while always ready to appreciate the power of Lessing's thought, could not regard his views of development within history as a real advance. And it is true that for Lessing history remained an immanent scheme, in which at most he was able to perceive a kind of progress within the history of the human race towards the desired goal of an entirely harmonious life of universal truths of reason. For Hamann progress was not a Christian conception at all. He spoke with the utmost scorn of the *Deus pædagogus* who had taken the place in Lessing's thought of the *summus philosophus* of the earlier *illuminati*.[1] Neither the immanent powers of man, nor the light of reason to guide him, provide an adequate description of man's life. Nature has joined man with God, through tradition and experience which are the means of revelation, and Lessing's interpretation is inadequate on two counts: it separates reason off from history, and it ascribes to God a merely immanent role in man's mind.

Hamann's view is surely nearer to the basic historical events of Christianity. The modern scholar, Rudolf Bultmann, both in his recent Gifford Lectures, *History and Eschatology*, and his earlier study, *Das Urchristentum*, shows a remarkable affinity at many

---

[1] R VI, 127-8 = N III, 310.

points with the views of Hamann. In his rejection of progress as a Christian norm, in his understanding of history as being the life of man concentrated in his present, and in his recognition of the *historical* transcendence of God as central to Christianity, he shows how the ideas of Hamann may bear fruit in our time. Thus Bultmann writes:

> In primitive Christianity the transcendence of God is radically conceived, and the Greek view is remote from it, namely, that God is immanent in the world, in so far as its order, the regular course of its happenings, and the natural powers which work in it, have a divine character.[1]

Again, he speaks flatly of the nineteenth century belief in progress as being opposed to the Christian faith,[2] of the meaning of history as lying " always in the present,"[3] not in the sense of " absolute ultimate knowledge,"[4] but in the sense that " the knowledge of history is at the same time self-knowledge."[5] Bultmann's positive view of the relation between history and eschatology can be summarised in his own words:

> It is the paradox of the Christian message that the eschatological event, according to Paul and John, is not to be understood as a dramatic cosmic catastrophe but as happening within history, beginning with the appearance of Jesus Christ, and in continuity with this occurring again and again in history, but not as the kind of historical development which can be confirmed by any historian. It becomes an event repeatedly in preaching and faith. Jesus Christ is the eschatological event not as an established fact of past time but as repeatedly present, as addressing you and me here and now in preaching.[6]

Neither for Bultmann nor for Hamann, therefore, can Lessing's

---

[1] *Das Urchristentum*, Zürich, 1949, 216.
[2] *History and Eschatology*, Edinburgh, 1957, 70. [3] Ibid., 155. [4] Ibid., 121.
[5] Ibid., 131. [6] Ibid., 151f.

view of the unfolding of human spirit, even under the guidance
of a divine Educator, be the revelation by which God speaks his
Word to man. The instruction of the Christian is not a sweetly
unfolding lesson, but a fearful wrestling till the dawn with the
stranger, the messenger of the Lord. And out of this wrestling
something new comes. For Hamann, history is unpredictable,
with chasms, and contradictions. But it is creative: it is a workshop, not a schoolroom. It is the new man of Christian faith who
is made in history:

> Man is therefore not only a living field, but also the son of
> the field, and not only field and seed (as in the system of the
> materialists and the idealists) but also the king of the field,
> who plants good seed and hostile tares in his field; for what is
> a field without seed, and a prince without land and produce?
> These three in us are therefore one, namely, God's field . . . .[1]

A compressed and somewhat cryptic summary of this kind of
historical eschatology may be found in Hamann's own words,
in the remarkable work, *Konxompax*:

> This unity of the head together with the division of the body
> into its members and their *differentia specifica* is the mystery of
> the kingdom of heaven from its genesis to its apocalypse—the
> burning point of all parables and types in the whole universe.. [2]

In our own words, the meaning of history is God's plan of
salvation. History is given a highly personal reference, as having
to do with man now, with man as God's creature. In the words
of Tage Schack:

> History for Hamann is not the mid-space between life's arising
> and its death, or a view of what has gone on in that space;

[1] R IV, 46 = N III, 40.   [2] R IV, 20 = N III, 226.

99

but it is this moment in which we now live, between birth and death, creation and judgment—and it is determined by these two.[1]

History is not process or development, but it is what goes on in us, what happens to us, now; and it is now, in the present, that we are all alike near to history's beginning and history's end. This centrality of man is not to be understood as a psychological reflection upon external events, and the reduction of their externality to immanence. But it is in response to God that man's history arises. We live with the origin of history, and with its end. A historical event is therefore a repetition or re-enactment of the whole story from Genesis to Apocalypse, that is, from our creation through the promise which has been fulfilled and on to the promise which is given to us in hope.

History for Hamann is therefore in a particular sense identical with mythology. The vast and mysterious creative and redemptive movement which is the substance of history provides countless signs and hints of our calling. It may therefore be read typologically, allegorically, parabolically. But at the same time it would be a one-sided reduction of Hamann's views to stop there. His view is indeed the opposite of what is currently considered to be the " mythological " interpretation of biblical history. Hamann does not suggest that we sink ourselves in the stories of the Bible, of Genesis, say, and by an imaginative effort transport ourselves into the age before the Fall, where all is unity and there is no break between the Word and the creation. Nor does he suggest that we regard the promise of the second coming, and the pictorial imagery of its presentation in the Apocalypse, as containing within themselves the only possible reality for our historical situation. Rather, he considers that in the myth we are invited to see our own present situation with its summons to

[1] Op. cit., 307.

response and responsibility. It is *there* that the burning point is to be found of all parables and types, in our personal response within our own historical, contingent life. History as myth therefore means for Hamann much more what we should have to describe to-day as Bultmann's *interpretation* of myth. The mythological account of the creation and of the second coming are alike descriptions of our present situation, our calling, of the judgment and the promise. That is to say, they are descriptions of God's action, which is at all times historical action, that is, a Word spoken and done into our present life. The clue lies in our personal life, and in the present recognition of all history as God's history. The mythological is simply a description, a sign or allegory, of our actual existence. That God has created *me* is the existential significance, for me, of the creation story. That I live under the promise and in hope is the existential significance, for me, of the second coming. To transpose this significance into any other would-be objective terms, or stubbornly to cling to the images *per se*, is to empty them of their historicity, and to edge man out of his central place, with God, in the whole story. The images are truly historical when they become signs for me in my present historical existence. History is not a mere picture-book; it is a living dialogue between God and human existence. It is not a series of links in a long chain, but a perfect moment, a *kairos*, in God's hands. Each moment, in the hands of providence, may become this *kairos*, for an individual, for a nation, for an age.

All Hamann's free allegorising and typological interest in the Bible is to be understood in this way, that is, as the means of facing biblical history as a present Word: for the divine word is the one clue to disclose to us a knowledge of history:[1]

The book of nature and the book of history are nothing but

---

[1] Cf. R I, 138 = N I, 303.

ciphers, hidden signs, which need the same key as unlocks Holy Scripture, and is the point of its inspiration.[1]

In conclusion, you understand the past from the present; but the present in turn is grasped from the future, that is, from God's future, the future which is in the hands of God, which is the only free and real future. God speaks to us from the end. History is his. Historical existence means openness to this future. We can never go outside history. Not even the signs of which history consists, the "silhouettes of more mysterious actions," can take us outside history. For the depth of the sign is in history, and we are constantly recalled to this history, that is, to our own existence. We discern the wholeness of history, but in faith, darkly, in fragments. "All our knowledge is in part."[2] The wholeness is beyond, transcendent: only in signs does it happen here in our midst. And if we are able to call history God's plan of salvation it is not as the consequence of any reasonable assurance, far less a proof inferred from a well-established argument or drawn from any sign of progress. But it is the meaning to be glimpsed and held in faith, in the presence of God's Spirit making us alive, and making us new.

R I, 148 = N I, 308.   [2] R VII, 68 = N III, 317.

6

FRUITION

WE HAVE now looked at Hamann's thought along the perspectives
opened up by his views on faith, on the Word, and on history.
At the beginning I said that his own life was his best composition.
Hegel said that Hamann's writings " do not so much have a
peculiar style, as that they are style through and through."[1]
If we add that here above all the style reflects the man, then we
can also say that the writings are mere casual windows through
which we may glimpse the life of the man. They are only
fragmentary if taken by themselves. But Hamann never desired
that his life as an author and his life as a man should be separated.
If you take the writings with the man, they fall into place.

Yet even this is not easily proved. For Hamann's life in the
worldly sense was a failure. When he sold a house he always lost
money. His only son caused him a good deal of sorrow, and for
his three daughters he found it impossible to provide an education.
His daily job was quite dissociated from his real interests: first as
a copyist and translator, and later as the manager of the Customs
warehouse, and always with an inadequate salary, later sharply
pruned by the cheeseparing regulations of Frederick the Great,
the " Solomon of the North," as Hamann called him, he lived a
life full of cares.

But he also knew all his life how to eat his bread with gladness
and drink his wine with a merry heart; for God approved what
he did. These words of Ecclesiastes were often in his mind.[2]
And with his household joys, and a host of friends with whom he

---

[1] Op. cit., 209.   [2] Ecclesiastes 9. 7.

was in correspondence all his life, it cannot be said that he was a neglected genius. Herder, Kant, Lavater, Karl Friedrich von Moser, Matthias Claudius, Fritz Jacobi, were among those who knew and respected and even loved him. It was an age of friendship, and Hamann kept his friendships in repair with an almost anxious delight. His letters combine the charm and unflagging care for detail of Cowper's effusions, with the wide scope and penetrating insights of Gray's scholarly letters.

In the last years of his life, however, there came a remarkable fruition to his patience and humility. First of all a wealthy young admirer of Hamann's, Franz Buchholtz, made a generous gift which freed him of financial worries in regard to the future of his children. With his health none too good, he sought leave of absence from his post, and after prolonged efforts received a cold and peremptory dismissal, with a pittance of a pension. Nevertheless, he was at last able, in the summer of 1787, to set off on a visit, accompanied by his son, to Buchholtz in Westphalia. The account of that time, till his death a year later, which is to be found in letters and diaries, is of a remarkable serenity and concentration, and may even be called a fruition of his whole life. Hamann himself felt this, for in spite of declining health he was able to write home, giving his address (Jacobi's estate of Pempelfort, near Düsseldorf) as " Elysium."

The circumstances were strange. He found himself in the midst of a circle of Roman Catholic priests, one of them, Fürstenberg, being vicar general and former prime minister of the prince-bishop of Münster. At the centre of the circle was a remarkable woman, the Princess Amalie von Gallitzin. She too was a Roman Catholic, the wife of a Russian diplomat who was ambassador to the Hague. She had retired to an estate near Münster in order to devote herself to the upbringing of her two children and to the deepening of her own spiritual life. She set herself to educate the children in full and conscious opposition to the spirit of the age in which she lived. And for herself she sought with passionate intensity for a life of Christian perfection. It is from her diaries that we have the fullest account of that year. Hamann's relations with her are an illustration, the only full illustration, and confirmation, of the conscious shaping which he had given to his whole life. In a sense she may be called his only true disciple. Brief though their time together was, she understood him as no one else did. But perhaps it is enough that one person could truly understand him, could penetrate the veil of his irony, the obscurity of his sibylline utterances, and in turn see herself and her Christian ambitions in their true light: this is perhaps confirmation enough of the reality of Hamann's achievement.

What did she find in him? I give the story so far as possible in her own words. First, from her diary nearly a year after Hamann's death:

Finally came Hamann and showed me the heaven of true humility and surrender—a child's attitude to God . . . All my other friends, not excepting Fürstenberg, had hitherto regarded my powerful impulse towards perfection as the best thing about me, indeed as something admirable and lovely . . . But Hamann saw pride in this, and told me so. In pointing this out he ripped the skin from my bones, I thought that my only crutch was being taken from me, the cripple, but I loved and honoured him too deeply not to accept his lesson in my soul . . . after his death there was a wonderful change in me, or rather this change continued in me which his company during his lifetime had begun in me . . .[1]

This humility which she perceived in Hamann was the chief sign of his character. It was a humility powerful enough to make a decisive change in her life. She suddenly saw, with the help of

[1] Quoted in Nadler, op. cit., 453.

Hamann's courageous simplicity, that the efforts she had hitherto made, with the help of her spiritual director Overberg and the approval and admiration of Fürstenberg, were misguided. The Christian way is not direct, and to strive for perfection, as she had done ever since her withdrawal from the life of the court and the world, is in fact to be guided by the concept of perfectionism drawn from that very world of the *Aufklärung* which she was seeking to overcome. Hamann saw the pride and self-love in which her humility was clothed. And she with his help saw it too.

At times, she confesses, she even found Hamann's humility exaggerated. But through it, she writes:

I experienced many a quickening moment . . . Once in particular I was so happy, and got with him, and through the sight of him, an exalted picture of a great Christian clothed in rags, of strength in weakness, which filled my soul with enthusiasm, but also bowed it down, since I saw the gulf which still lay between me and that greatness, and my bowing was not pride. For no form can be more opposed to pride than this in every sense true servant's form, which, briefly, is nothing less than a complete turning inside out, where that which a man usually bears on the outside goes inside, and what he usually conceals within him he now exposes. Oh, only he who can do this wholly is wholly a Christian! Now as soon as this lovely picture of " divine blessedness " comes into my mind, there arises in my longing for it a glowing flame—and soon afterwards, how helplessly far I am from it! Once again I am busy with my usual stuff, and worrying about vain things. Disbelief in the truth, or rather doubt of the truth together with an easy belief which is equivalent to self-deceit, these inseparable symptoms (as Hamann calls them)—how do I get saved from these evils? What is truth? What truth do I know, can I know, as truth? Only one, believe in the Lord, love him, and hope for his day.[1]

In these last words she, the earnest Catholic, is clearly echoing the words of Hamann, the good Lutheran. For Hamann holiness is a gift from God, received in faith, the beginning of the Christian life, not the goal of an immense process of self-discipline and self-education.[2] The consequence for the Christian in his relation with others is again indirectness, a life of concealment. This the Princess Gallitzin clearly sees at work in Hamann's life, as the deliberate expression of his humility. Thus a little later she writes:

> He continually shows himself almost as a fool . . . He never tries to shine and please others in his opinions and remarks, or to captivate others.[3]

She sees, too, that the reality in this inversion, this concealment, this self-abasement, consists in its being always in relation to God, and not to the mere kaleidoscope of the inward life. The cultivation of the inward life as a thing in itself is quite excluded by the nature of its impulse from God. Elsewhere Hamann speaks of " the infinite mis-relation of man to God,"[4] and it is this combination of the nothingness of man with the infinite grace of God which determines the nature of Hamann's faith and life. Thus she writes, in her account of Hamann's death:

> Something important of Hamann's spirit and teaching has remained in my soul, the conviction, namely, that the effort to attain to a good conscience, since man should not know if he deserves hatred or love, was a very dangerous ferment in

---

[1] *Briefwechsel und Tagebücher der Fürstin Amalie von Gallitzin*, Neue Folge, Münster, 1876, III, 330-1.
[2] Cf. F. Blanke, op. cit., 116.   [3] Op. cit., 351.
[4] R VII, 59 = N III, 312; and 230, below.

me; and that the chief thing in faith must be the enduring of my nothingness and complete confidence in God's mercy. I had a living impression at that time—but only after a long struggle with Hamann—that my pleasure in the bitter dislike of my own imperfection and weakness was actually the most secret and perilous hiding-place of my pride. Not without a struggle and tears did I let go of this last position of my pride, and that only in spirit and not at all yet in deed. But I have seen it, and Thou O God give me Thy grace to finish the struggle, that is, to bear my own lowliness with patience to the end. Amen.[1]

So the way of indirectness triumphed in her, and its presentation by Hamann also in indirectness is confirmed as a way of real communication between two people. Amalie von Gallitzin, the devout and troubled Catholic soul, finds in the words and style of the most thoroughgoing Lutheran of his age the invitation she requires. This is a true ecumenical encounter, involving a real unity in Christ, of a kind that is vainly sought to-day through the mere manipulation of doctrine and order. She recognises that his withholding of himself is part of the necessary witness. It is not he himself, but the divine folly and weakness, which he points out to her, while he himself remains in weakness and concealment. So again she notes:

When he has expressed an opinion which strikes home to other people, he takes up the opposite view, when he sees that his first opinion is passionately espoused.[2]

And again:

He himself shuns nothing so much as to appear virtuous or learned; his humility is as artless as Fürstenberg's righteousness

... He speaks proudly, and shows himself to be humble. False humility does the reverse.[1]

This is the irony of the true Christian witness. He points away from himself, he makes himself small, he even makes himself appear different from what he is, so that there can be no boasting at all, no reliance upon anything he is in himself.

That this inversion was not a casual expression of Hamann's last year, but a deliberate discipline, may be gathered from the reference in a letter, written to F. E. Lindner on Easter Day, 1783, in which he speaks of the duty and the art of this kind of concealment:

A strict morality seems to me to be more contemptible and shallower than the most wilful scoffing and mockery. To drive the good deep inside, to drive the evil to the outside, to seem worse than one really is, to be really better than one seems: this I consider to be both a duty and an art.[2]

Hamann's whole authorship, indeed, as well as his life, may be regarded as an exercise in this kind of concealment. Not a single piece appeared under his own name, and in this he exceeds in indirectness even the authorship of Kierkegaard. Kierkegaard, indeed, was much more self-conscious and romantic in his pseudonymic acrobatics. And he deliberately published, simultaneously with his pseudonymous writings, a series of " direct " writings, for edification, under his own name. The difference between the two is not superficial, as we have already seen.[3] For Hamann the duty and art of concealment expresses his conviction that directness is never possible, that the witness can never point to his own achievement, that humour is therefore the final stage, even in faith. For Kierkegaard " humour is the

---

[1] Ibid., 351. [2] R VI, 339. [3] See above, 18ff.

last stage of the inwardness of existence before faith."[1] Of a piece with Hamann's conviction is his remark that he preferred, when he went to church, to hear the truth from a poor preacher rather than a popular preacher. Kierkegaard recognised this as a true expression of the " humour which contains a much deeper scepticism than irony,"[2] and quoted with approval Hamann's remark that he would rather hear the truth from Balaam's ass than from the wisest master.[3] The point at which Hamann and Kierkegaard part company is precisely that where Kierkegaard, wishing to come out into the open, walks into a wilderness of his own making; whereas Hamann, remaining in the world, knows that in doing so he is at the same time a voice crying in the wilderness. But it is the wilderness which is at the same time full of hints and signs of our calling.

Hamann's " humour," that is to say, is bound up with a radical pessimism, or more precisely, a Christian realism about the condition of man: you can be a Christian only in rags, you have really nothing. As the Princess Gallitzin records, Hamann says:

Ma seule règle, c'est de n'en point avoir. My sole rule is to have none. All the good we human beings are capable of is merely negative; whether in relation to ourselves or others. We can only strive to remove what prevents us from seeing more clearly, and presenting, the influence of the Godhead

(and she adds, with immense penetration into Hamann's way)

---

[1] *Gesammelte Werke*, VI, Jena, 1910, 362 (quoted in *Hamanns Hauptschriften erklärt*, I, 49).

[2] *Samlede Verke*, XIII, 393.

[3] The " Balaam's ass " reference I have not been able to discover—if indeed it ever existed outside Kierkegaard's imagination. Even Kierkegaard's own reference in his Journal (*Papirer*, II, A, 12) only says that Hamann writes this " at one point." The more general reference, however, is as follows: " I have not yet heard your brother-in-law preaching, and I no longer seek out a preacher, but content myself with him whom God gives. Baumgarten, Forstmann, Reichel, Paul and Cephas are men, and I more often hear, with more joy, the Word of God in the mouth of a Pharisee, as a witness against his will, than from the mouth of an angel of light." (R. I, 497 = B I, 431, letter to Lindner, 12 October, 1759.)

—a striving for systemlessness, for no system, and for the Socratic, simple and lofty consciousness of our ignorance, frailty and weakness. He who attains this will be without any great strain humble, long-suffering, and therefore loving with his whole heart, and will possess the peace which passes understanding.[1]

This is the patience and receptivity of the Christian man, expecting nothing from men, and giving nothing to men, but living in the freedom which comes from God, and in " the love with which Christ loved men, but without striving for love and enjoyment from others in return."[2] This is not a recoil from the moral life, or a retreat into the nothingness of the mystic. But it is the true setting for a life of Christian love. It is an existential attitude to the Word and action of God, which sets our existence in the light of the truth. When this is done, we may be filled with hope and peace.

In Hamann's words, which made all the greater impression on the Princess Gallitzin because they were spoken in her presence, one day in November 1787, during a ridiculous difference of opinion between Hamann and the sensitive and over-anxious Buchholtz:

If I sow a seed in the earth, I do not stand around and listen and watch to see if it grows, but I sow and go away and sow somewhere else, and I leave to God the growth and the increase.[3]

It is to the Princess Gallitzin that we owe the touching description of Hamann's last days. She writes in her diary:

Thursday the 19th [June 1788] was the last morning I spent with the dear, blessed man. I had breakfast with him, he was very weak. I had indeed seen him in this state before, and

---

[1] Op. cit., 351.   [2] Quoted in Blanke, op. cit., 120.   [3] Gallitzin, op. cit., III, 101.

ascribed it, as he did, to the unrest of the last few weeks, the trouble and fatigue with B. [Buchholtz]; and I really believed this. As soon as he got into the coach to travel to Düsseldorf he would change, and recover as marvellously quickly as he always did... The pipe which was waiting for him in the case gave him a childish joy, and especially my name, and the year, engraved on it. "You want me to remember you always," he said, with his eyes full of tears. "I have reason enough without this." I: "Pray sometimes for your daughter, and when you write do not call me Your Excellency." He: "No, I prefer to call you Amalie. My prayer is worth nothing. But we all have an Intercessor, who pleads for us with sighs unceasingly." ——"When Hans goes out to-day, you will be alone. Do you want Mikelu or P. etc.?"—"No, I need nothing, and I am never alone. Nor will you ever be alone. We have One who is always with us and in us" (with tears). ——I seized his hands with inexpressible grief, and kissed them long. ——"You humble me, dear Amalie." ... We spoke much about our favourite object, the Bible ... Among other things he said of unworthy communicating, and the parable of the wedding garment: "Everything must be given to us, that we may communicate worthily, as the wedding garment was given to the guests in the old custom. The will is the only thing we can add." Concerning the parable of the children playing in the market-place and whistling to one another, he said, that it should be understood of the people who were able to suck poison from the best—whom therefore we could never make right.

When it was about ten o'clock and I had to go, I became inexpressibly anxious. He noticed it, and repeatedly begged me not to bid good-bye, he wanted to wait for me in Düsseldorf till the end of June, though his son, who had come in again, very roughly disagreed with him, and he mildly opposed him, and, as his son spoke of being wrong, somewhat reluctantly added: " My son, I can certainly be wrong, and it can happen to you too: *errare humanum est . . .*" [1]

A little less than a month previously, on 22 May, they had been sitting together in the arbour——

Last Thursday the 22nd, as I sat with him in the arbour after our meal, I was very moved when he quoted, with the fullness of feeling which is only possible to one to whom this feeling is quite his own, the words from Paul about the divine folly, I Corinthians, 1. 23, 25, 27. I had to force back the tears which rose to my eyes, for I felt him at that moment to be veiled livingly in these words. His weaknesses may be legion; I have never seen a weakness in him without being filled with fresh reverence; for he never covered them over, or softened them when he became aware of them and of his watchers. He *does* have childish outbursts, especially against his own son; but I never once saw him frightened by the regard of witnesses, or trying to change his gall into sweetness. [2]

He died on 21 June, 1788, and was buried in the Princess's garden in Münster. On his tombstone she had engraved the words of St. Paul in which she had felt that his whole life was concealed:

Nos autem prædicamus Christum crucifixum: Judæis quidem scandalum, gentibus autem stultitiam. Quia quod stultum est Dei, sapientius est hominibus: et quod infirmum est Dei, fortius est hominibus.

The dedication was *Johanni Georgio Hamanno viro Christiano.*

[1] Op. cit., III, 354-9.   [2] Op. cit., III, 352.

Selected Writings

BIBLICAL REFLECTIONS

1758

These are the immediate jottings of Hamann's intensive reading of the Bible in London in the spring of 1758. There is space only for a fraction of the material available. Exegetical, reflective and personal interests are all present, and in the selection I have tried to represent this variety.

BIBLICAL REFLECTIONS

I HAVE begun to-day with God's help to read Holy Scripture through for the second time. Since my circumstances impose upon me the utmost solitude, in which I sit and watch like a sparrow on the roof-top, I find an antidote to the bitterness of sad reflections upon my past follies, upon my misuse of the kindness and the opportunities with which Providence so graciously singled me out, in the company of my books, and in the employment and exercise which they give to my thoughts. The prospect of a barren desert, in which I see myself deprived of water and nourishment, is nearer to me now than ever before. The sciences and the friends of my reason seem, like Job's, more to try my patience than to give me comfort, and more to open the wounds of my experience than to ease their pain. Nature has put a salt into every body, which the analysts can extract, and Providence, it seems, has put a primal moral element into all adversities, which we are to release and separate off, and which we can profitably use as a help in the sicknesses of our nature and the illnesses of our spirit. If we fail to see God in the sunshine in the pillar of cloud, then in the pillar of fire by night his presence is more visible and emphatic. If I look back on my whole life I am justified in having the greatest confidence in his grace. Even in my present state I recognise a loving father warning me by earnest glances, who has let me come to myself, like the prodigal son, and will answer my penitent return to him not only by withholding the punishment I deserve, but also by graciously forgiving me and welcoming me against all expectation. Neither my evil will nor the opportunity was lacking that I should fall into far deeper misery and far heavier debts than I am in at present. God! we are such poor creatures that we must even be thankful to thee when our wickedness is less than it might be! God! we are such unworthy creatures that nothing but our unbelief can shorten thine arm, and set limits to thy generous blessing!

... The great author of these holy books intends to make every honest reader of them wise unto salvation through faith in his Redeemer. The holy men under whose names the books have been preserved were impelled by the Holy Spirit: divine inspiration was imparted to them as they prepared their writings, that they might be profitable to us for doctrine, reproof, correction and instruction in righteousness (II Tim. 3. 15-16 and II Pet. 1. 21). God cannot withdraw this effect from anyone who prays for it, since the Holy Spirit is promised to all who ask the heavenly Father for it. The necessity we are under, as readers, to put ourselves in the place of the particular author before us, to feel his feelings and as far as possible enter into his attitude, with the aid of imaginative powers which a poet or historian himself helps to awake in us, is a rule which applies just as much here as with other books.

I now offer some general remarks, as they occur to me, about divine revelation. God has revealed himself to man in nature and in his Word. The resemblances and the connections between these two revelations have not yet been sufficiently discussed or clearly explained, nor pushed to that point of harmony which might open up a broad field for a sound philosophy. In countless instances both revelations must be rescued from the greatest objections in an identical way. Both revelations explain and support one another, and cannot contradict one another, however much the explanations of our reason would like to show contradictions. Rather, it is the greatest contradiction and abuse of reason when reason itself tries to *reveal*. A philosopher who ignores the divine Word in order to please reason is like the Jews who, the more firmly they seem to cling to the Old Testament, the more stubbornly they reject the New Testament. In them was the prophecy fulfilled that what should have served to confirm and to fulfil their other insights is a stumbling-block and foolishness in their eyes. Natural science and history are the two things on which true religion rests. Unbelief and superstition are based on shallow physics and shallow history. Nature is as little subject to blind chance or to eternal laws as all events are to be derived from personalities and reasons of state. A Newton will be equally moved as a natural scientist by God's wise omnipotence and as a historian by God's wise government.

God reveals himself—the Creator of the world an author—what a fate his books must undergo, to what strict judgments and sharp-witted critics they will be subject! How many pitiful scoffers of religion have enjoyed their daily bread at his hands; how many strong spirits, like Herostratus, have in their daring sought one kind of immortality, and in their fear of death have implored a better!

God is accustomed to have his wisdom impugned by the children of men. Moses's rod was in no danger, even though he was surrounded by the hissing rods of the wise Egyptians. These sorcerers were finally compelled to see the finger of God in the meanest vermin and to yield to the prophet of the true God. The idea that the supreme being himself has honoured men with a special revelation seems so strange and extraordinary to the wits that with Pharaoh they ask what this God desires, and what is his commandment. But this idea of revelation must be considered in connection with those for whose good it happened. God desired to reveal himself to *men*; he revealed himself *through men*. The means of making this revelation useful for men, winning them for it, and propagating and preserving it among them, had to be appropriately based by God upon the nature of men and upon his own wisdom. A philosopher who desired to blame or to improve upon God in the choice of all these circumstances and ways of communicating revelation would be acting more rationally if he trusted his own judgment less, and avoided the danger into which the royal astronomer fell who identified the Ptolemaic system or his own explanation of the movements of the stars with the true structure of the heavens.

If God intended to reveal himself to men and the whole human race, then the folly of those is even more striking who try to make their own limited taste and their own judgment the touchstone of the divine Word. We have not to do with a revelation which a Voltaire, a Bolingbroke or a Shaftesbury might find acceptable, which might best satisfy their prejudices, their wit, their moral, political and magical fancies, but with a disclosure of truths whose certainty, credibility and rightness concern the whole human race. People who credit themselves with insight enough of their own, to enable them to dispense with divine instruction, would have found mistakes in any other revelation, and have no need of one. They are the healthy who need no physician.

God indisputably found it most appropriate to his wisdom to bind this nearer revelation of himself first to a single man, then to his family, and finally to a particular people, before he allowed it to become more general. We can no more investigate the reasons for this choice than ask why it pleased God to create in six days that which his will could just as well have realised in a single instant of time.

Further, God condescended as much as possible to human inclinations and ideas, even to prejudices and weaknesses. This special characteristic of his love for men, of which the whole of Scripture is full, gives grounds for mockery to weak minds which presuppose in the divine Word human wisdom, or satisfaction for their curiosity, their wit, and agreement with the taste of the time in which they live or with the sect they belong to. No wonder if they find themselves deceived in their ideas, and if the spirit of Scripture is rejected by them with the same indifference, and as seeming to be just as dumb and useless as the Saviour did to Herod, who, despite his great curiosity and expectation, soon sent him back to Pilate with something more than cold indifference.

Who could have imagined that men would want to look for a history of the world in the Pentateuch? Many people seem to revile Moses merely because he does not give them the means to explain, supplement or refute the fables of Herodotus. How ludicrous and unbelievable such a history of the early world would probably seem to them, if we did have it as fully as they would like!

These books were to be preserved by the Jews. Many particular circumstances in them had therefore to concern this people so closely that they were really interested in their content. The history of this people is in itself of greater importance with regard to our religion than the history of any other people; since God has presented, in the stubbornness of this nation, the saddest picture of our corrupt nature, and in his guiding and governing of it the greatest proofs of his patience, justice and mercy—in brief, the most sensible revelations of his qualities.

Why did God choose this people? Not on account of their good qualities. The free-thinkers may make as much play as they like with their stupidity and their wickedness compared with other peoples. Did God not will to transmit the gospel by means of instruments that were ignorant and unimpressive in the eyes of the world? Who can fathom his decree?

Little though Voltaire and Bolingbroke found in the first five chapters of Genesis to supplement and explain primitive history, its disclosures are nevertheless of great importance for the human race as a whole.

There has been among the philosophers no lack of good will to explain the creation as a natural event. It is therefore no wonder that they have attributed the same idea to Moses, instead of expecting a story from him. A story to be judged by the idea of the time, which must to some extent be related to the ideas of the time in which he wrote, can give little satisfaction to those who are looking for an explanation, who prefer that a thing should be comprehensible rather than true. We know how many follies have been perpetrated through the inclination to explore the future. We know that this inclination has given man the confidence that he is capable of it, and that he possesses the proper and adequate means for it in the stars, the flight of birds, etc.— thus satisfying his own presumption. The curiosity to know things which are too high for us, which are beyond our horizon, which are unfathomable precisely because of the weakness which makes the future so obscure to us, has led men into many such ludicrous methods and errors. Such people have been called sages and philosophers with as much right as gipsies, astrologers, etc. have been called prophets.

Let us compare natural events with natural events and miracles with miracles, if we are to make a judgment about them.

It would be as ludicrous to ask Moses to explain nature with the aid of Aristotelian, Cartesian or Newtonian concepts as to expect God to have revealed himself in the general philosophical language which has been the philosophers' stone for so many learned minds.

To say that Moses wrote only for the mob is either meaningless or ridiculous. Does the sun rise so early in the summer for the farmer alone, because the lazy townsman and the voluptuous courtier can do without it for so many hours more, or indeed do without it altogether?

Paul was transported, he could find no words to recount clearly the ideas which he brought back with him from the third heaven. Just as our ears cannot hear till they are touched by sound from the air, and all intelligible hearing depends upon a vibration of the air which is neither too powerful nor too weak, so it is with our ideas. They depend on physical images, and where these are lacking or where we cannot awake identical images in others [there is no communication]. We see how difficult it is to translate the figures and idioms of one language into another, and the more the way of thought of two peoples differs, the more we are forced into deviations and substitutes or verbal equivalents. Therefore of what nature must a story be in which things are to be made clear and comprehensible to us which lie too far beyond the scope of our ideas?

With what humility, silent attentiveness and deep reverence we must accept what the Creator of the world wishes to make known to us of the mysteries of the great week in which he worked at our earth. Short though the story is of the creation of a being that met with his approval when it came into existence, and which he has found worthy of preservation so long, reserving it as a mere scaffolding for a higher structure to be erected in the most ceremonious fashion, yet this story must be important in our eyes. Deep as his condescension is to make known to us the little that it is possible, necessary and useful for us to understand, so high does he surpass our powers of thought.

Genesis 1

What a disclosure in the nature of man! How ceremoniously does the triune God prepare himself, before he undertakes the fashioning of man! How often does Moses, and the Spirit of God through him, find it necessary to repeat this assurance that God has created man in his own image, in the image of God, after the divine likeness. Here reason sinks down, and it is on this basis that the decision of God rests to save fallen man, to restore this image. How much it has cost that I am saved! Unfathomable God, thou hast nevertheless considered this race worthy of the costly ransom. And that we are so worthy in our salvation is due to the worth which thou hast ascribed and communicated to us in creation. To restore this likeness God had to assume the likeness of men. Both are equally great mysteries of faith.

Subdue the earth (Psalm 115. 16). Be gods of the earth. Maintain in your world the holiness which dwells with us in heaven. Assert your dominion in the dignity which we have given to you in creation especially over the creatures subordinate to you. Spirits which would never have received their being if God had not given it to them, rebelled against his throne and forfeited their bliss; beware lest your subjects exercise the cunning, power or evil against you that came to grief against the deity; beware of those creatures who are there for your sake.

Reason must be satisfied with the judgment of that philosopher upon the writings of Heraclitus: what I understand is excellent, so I infer the same about what I do not understand. Only God's own witness can fully assure us, where our own insight into nature is inadequate. God made this judgment after he looked at every part of creation: each part was good. The connection of all the parts gives them the supreme good and perfection. " And God saw everything that he had made, and behold, it was very good " (Gen. 1. 31).

" God created and made." Matter and form. Both existence and destiny, so that nothing becomes something, and this something becomes all that he wills. How can we express in words that which we cannot in the least imagine? We must regard ourselves as those who are deaf from birth and are laboriously taught to utter certain words whose impression they cannot hear, and who to some extent, by watching other people's lips, replace their deafness by sight.

The forming of man, as described by Moses, gives us a standard by which to judge our nature. Wonderfully constructed though our body is, God as it were neglects to remind man of his own wisdom in this work, but thinks it more necessary to draw his attention to the dust of the earth, from which he made this masterpiece of the physical world. It seems to be for this reason that Moses uses for the creation of the firmament the common and neutral image of lights. He even dwells on the matter, when he speaks of the sun and the moon as two great lights, " the greater light to rule the day, and the lesser light to rule the night," in order to keep the Jews safe from a natural idolatry of the stars, and especially of those which are most apparent. I suppose this observation has been made before; it shows how God adapts himself in his revelation to human ideas and to the times, and has looked to the general profit in the use of the little circumstances which some find derisory. If then this body of ours is dust, with what love and care should we treat it! God has created from dust such a miraculous structure, a mirror of the macrocosm, as our Lord in his first miracle made wine out of water which was better than the first wine ...

Genesis 3

Fear, the shame of a bad conscience, the folly and the inadequacy of our reason to make good and to cloak the evil of our heart, are depicted in this part of the story with a fidelity, simplicity and profundity of which no human pen would have been capable. The difficulties of understanding the circumstances of the fall flow from prejudices about the wisdom of Adam, and from false conceptions of the wisdom of God. This is the childhood of the human race, in which consisted its innocence, in which God would have preserved it, in which he would have brought up his creatures till they reached the glorious height of the faith which our Saviour compared to a mustard-seed growing into a perfect tree. The uneasiness of a bad conscience is like the movements we call shame and fear. We must set aside all secondary notions, and regard the motions of the soul alone; our words are allegories or images of our thoughts . . .

Genesis 4. 9

God appears here as a judge for the second time. Just as he asked Adam, Where art thou? he now asks Cain, Where is Abel, thy brother? Just as Adam combined ingratitude with his disobedience of God, so his son combined lies with the murder. The rebel against society received forgiveness, as the rebel against God had received it. The death-sentence, which both had deserved, was not carried out. The commandments of the second tables of the law were based upon the first. Hence unbelief and superstition destroy all the security and peace of human society. Unbelief is the theoretical, superstition the practical enemy of mankind. The heathen temples were full of unbelieving idolaters; our times have produced fanatics of unbelief who pay homage to reason as only the papists do to Mary.

Genesis 5—6. 3

When we consider the constitution of our body and the number of years we live, it seems that the body's frailty and weakness is proportionate to the years. The genealogy in this chapter shows, however, how long the first men lived compared with us. It shows also how everything in the course of nature and its laws is directly dependent on God. What law of nature is more general and more certain than that man must die? Even this law is waived by the will of the Highest in the case of Enoch. Just as men often oppose their nature to their reason and will, and turn their customary actions into necessities, so worldly wisdom has often tried to oppose nature to its creator, and spoken of anti-natural and supernatural works. How many miracles has God done, one should rather say, so that we should look upon nothing as natural; and what is there in nature, in the commonest and most natural events, that is not a miracle for us in the strictest sense?

Genesis 27

It is astonishing to see how God enters into every little circumstance, and prefers to reveal his rule in common events of human life rather than in rare and extraordinary events; how he holds men's prejudices, errors, and good and bad inclinations in his power, leads them by his counsel and, notwithstanding all human hindrances, gloriously fulfils them as it were in and through themselves. While we poor ignorant men think of nothing but our little passions and projects, how we may satisfy the passions, and carry out the projects, God deals us his own plan, at which a Rebecca works as at her own, and an Isaac, despite his reluctance, and his circumspection lest he be deceived, must put his hand to the same plan. It was in vain that Isaac trembled very exceedingly, that he was seized by one violent shudder after the other—" I have blessed him: yea, and he shall be blessed." It was in vain that Esau, who despised his birthright, now saw the greatness of the blessing he had deprived himself of.

Deuteronomy 4

What a splendid chapter! Every word that proceeds from the mouth of God is a whole creation of thoughts and movements in our soul: wisdom and understanding, which the devils will envy and respect us for, if we keep the commandments. In spite of the light which God sheds in our souls by his Word, he wants to be near to us himself. He is where his Word is, he is where his Son is. If his Word is in us, his Son is in us; if his Word is in us, the Spirit of this Word is in us. How could God the Father do without us when we robbed him of his best company? He leaves heaven, he makes it deserted and empty, and comes into our hearts not only to make a paradise of them, as of the waste and empty earth, but to pitch the tent of heaven itself. O how holy should this lump of earth be to us on which God deigns to set his tabernacle because our poor spirit dwells beneath it. Praise be to God from everlasting to everlasting, Amen.

VERSE 39. The whole duration of time is nothing but a to-day of eternity. The whole of time made up a single day in God's economy in which all hours cohere and are included in one morning and one evening. The coming of our Saviour was the noon-day of time. The creation which cost God six days shall not last longer than to-day. God! what is eternity, and what is the Lord of eternity! How many millions of days it has taken, how many millions of revolutions the earth has made before it has reached to-day's; and how many millions will follow which Thou hast numbered as all that have passed have been numbered. Just as this eternity of days which have been and will be in the world are nothing but to-day for Thee, so is the present day an eternity for me, even the present moment is an eternity for me. Lord, thy Word makes us wise, even if it teaches us nothing more than to number our days. What a nothingness, mere smoke, a spiritual nothingness they are in our eyes when reason numbers them! What a fullness, what a treasure, what an eternity, when faith numbers them! Lord, teach me to number my days, that I may apply my heart to wisdom. All is wisdom in thy ordering of nature, when the spirit of thy Word illumines our spirit. All is a labyrinth and disorder when we try to look for ourselves.

We are more miserable than blind when we despise thy Word and look at nature through Satan's deceiving glasses. Our eyes have the sharpness of the eagle's and the light of the angels when we see everything in thy Word—thyself, loving God, and heaven and earth, the richness of both, the work of thy hands, the thoughts of thy heart towards both and in both.

The Christian alone is a man, a father, lord of the animals. He alone loves himself, his own and his goods, because he loves God who loved him before he was, and, when he was, was God's enemy. My Lord and my God!

Lengthen the days of thy life—is man omnipotent that he can do this? Does God regard us for his own sake? How wise of God to hide the future from us, since we know nothing of the world to come. The Christian alone is lord of his days, because he is heir to the future. Our time is so bound up with eternity that one cannot separate them without extinguishing the light of their life. However dissimilar in their nature, their union is the soul of human life, as the union of the soul and the body consti-tutes temporal life.

Joshua 1. 18

Here we find a new example of how God commands in advance what man, when left to himself, sees as necessary and as his duty. Hence in the abyss of our heart there is a voice which Satan himself does not let us hear, but which God hears, and which he also tries to draw our attention to. When we reach self-know-ledge, when it happens that we see ourselves in our true form, how we desire, and plead, and are anxious, how we feel the necessity of all that God, without our knowledge or participation or interest, has never wearied to hold before us, to offer to us, and to encourage us, even to frighten us, into accepting. Then we hear in our heart the blood of the Reconciler crying; we feel

that it is sprinkled with the blood that was shed for the reconcilia-
tion of the whole world, that the vengeance cries for grace.
All the miracles of Holy Scripture take place in our soul. Great
God, our spoiled nature, in which thou didst desire to unite and
create heaven and earth, is only too like chaos in being without
form, void, and dark, hiding from our eyes the depths which are
known to thee alone . . . Make this desert by the spirit of thy
mouth and by thy word into a good and fruitful land, a garden
of thy hand.

I Chronicles 12. 32

Understanding of the times provides us with the understanding
of our duties. The Lord of time alone knows time; therefore he
alone can tell us how important the moment is which he gives us.
The present moment is only a dead torso, without head or feet;
it simply lies where it is. The past must be revealed to us, and
the future likewise. In regard to the past our fellow-creatures
can help us somewhat; the future is completely closed to us:
even the breath of the succeeding hour is its own master, at least
it depends on its predecessor as little as it can command its
neighbour and successor. Every moment of time is perfectly
rounded; that out of each moment a line comes, is due to the
thread which Providence has drawn through it and which gives
it an exact connexion, which our weak eyes cannot see. This
thread makes the connexion of moments and parts of time so
firm and inseparable, so grown into one another, that everything consists, and seems to consist, of one piece.

Nahum

Next to the riches of God in nature, which arose out of nothing,
there is no greater creation than that of human conceptions and

experiences of heavenly and divine mysteries; the sovereign power of human language to penetrate to the thoughts of the cherubim and seraphim. How the sense-impressions swell and glow, rising to an intoxicating fervour, to the feeling and sight of faith and the spirit. Every single grape of the divine word is a whole wine-harvest for a Christian. All miracles are daily events, hourly experiences of the life in God. It is as impossible for a Christian to doubt God's word as for a baptised heathen to believe in it. It is more than the witness of the senses and of reason which belongs to religion. Religion needs a sounder seal than the applause of those immature and corrupt guardians who tell us what they see in their sleep.

Luke 10: The Good Samaritan:
Thoughts on the meaning of this parable

Its purpose is to show the nature of faith. Faith disposes of all self-righteousness and is based simply on the love of a redeemer. Faith in this redeemer can make us fruitful for good works, give us power to fulfil the law or to love our neighbour.

That this parable has to do with the redemption of the human race may be deduced from the question with which our Saviour makes the application. Who is your neighbour, O man, O sinner, O Christian? Who was it who showed you mercy when you lay in your blood, when the first-born of creation, like Cain, made the earth drink of it? Is it not your God who is your husband? (Isaiah 54. 5.) Is this not the first relation which man had to himself and to his creator? Is it not the closest relation? Did God not leave heaven and all things, in order to cling to his wife, did he not share her fate, her poverty, her sin and shame?

Was not Jesus cursed as a Samaritan for your sake—and as one of us? Did he not become a traveller for your sake—and with what discomforts—did he not come to where you were, see you

like Adam under the trees, like Nathanael under the fig-tree, have
pity on you—and not only come to where you were but go up
to you, even to you, bind up your wounds (I am the Lord that
healeth thee, Ex. 15. 26, did not the most distinctive signs of his
life consist in fulfilling this word and did a single disease or a
legion of demons ever make this word powerless?), pour in oil
and wine, both daughters of his own wine-presses, the fruits of his
righteousness, which alone can still your pains and cleanse your
wounds? Did you have strength to come to him of yourself, and
go to the refuge, the inn that he sought out and prepared for you?
He lends you his strength, which is not the strength of an earthly
king. The God of Israel takes no pleasure in horses or strong legs;
he lends you the beast on which he himself made his entry as a
humble and gentle king. He pays, he pleads and cares for you,
even when he has departed, he promises to return, and he frees
you from all your future debts. . . . Faith is the hand that takes
everything from Jesus and gives everything to him. I am the
half-dead traveller who has none other to thank for his life but
the merciful bearer of sins. Not the priest, or the Levite, but the
Samaritan in my breast, he himself, fashioned by the Holy Spirit
in my soul, will pour his oil and wine into the wounds, and tend
him in the humiliation in which I find him in the soul of my
neighbour. As everything, heaven and earth, was made by him
and for him, so everything in us comes from him and flows back
to him.

Our Saviour is therefore the true neighbour whom faith alone
can teach us to love. He is ascended, yet with us always, till the
end of the world. We do not have him himself with us, but the
poor we have always with us, and in them he waits for mercy
from us—that same mercy which he showed to us. He is so near
us that nothing can separate us from him: bone of our bone,
flesh of our flesh. Gratitude for what the Saviour has done for
us, the feeling of our corruption, the enjoyment of his grace,

abolishes our enmity with God. Since every man bears his image there is hatred and fratricide among men. The mercy we have received through Jesus, while we were yet enemies, shows us our neighbour as an image of ourself, as a creature in whom the Saviour who has saved us has the same interest. What you do to the least of these (a cup of cold water in my name) you do to me. Christ is therefore our neighbour—the one who has showed us mercy, whom we must love as ourselves because he died in our stead, because he lives in us, and we have been buried and are risen again with him.

To win eternal life we must do what he has done—show mercy. Mercy to every man, he lives in the least of men (he is the second Adam). He lives as a stranger, as a sick man, as an infant persecuted by Herod.

John 12. 29

" The crowd standing by heard the voice and said that it had thundered. Others said, An angel has spoken to him."

How the slightest circumstances are prophetic in Holy Scripture! Here we see human reason straying in two ways, which have persisted to our own time: explaining the voice of God by natural effects or by subordinate miracles. Rather than see and believe God, men imagine thunder or an angel. At the same time this is the effect which the revelation of God would have upon sinners and pious people. The unbeliever will hear a thunderclap, when the believer and the Christian hears angels' voices speaking to him.

Acts 17. 2

" Now all the Athenians and the foreigners who lived there

spent their time in nothing except telling or hearing something new."

Curiosity is a kind of superstition and idolatry. Socrates, whom the wise of the world have united to call a wise man, confessed that he knew nothing. Solomon, to whom the spirit of God ascribed this title with more justification, has left us in Ecclesiastes a testimony which is even more depressing. Nothing new . . . a sorrow and vexation and nausea to be wise. The father of modern philosophy found it necessary to forget, deny and reject all he knew, and regarded this as the only way to find the truth. But this truth was nothing but a structure of errors polished up anew and taken for new. If curiosity is the mother or foster-mother of knowledge, we can easily judge the fruits from the root and the sap. All natural knowledge is revealed. The nature of objects provides the material, and the laws by which our soul feels, thinks, infers, judges and compares, provide the form. Thus all natural knowledge is as old as nature itself, and since nature does not change there can be nothing new, in a real sense, in the experiencing of nature. To call part of the earth the new world is a palpable example of the misunderstanding in our ideas which is caused by our use of language, or rather of the falsifying of words by the weakness and ambiguity of our thoughts. This is the kind of deceit which makes us pass base coin as genuine. Therefore it is not in the course of nature or in the ambit of our reason or of any reasonable creature that we meet anything new: but what is new must take place outside this domain. Either God must change the course of nature, or give us another horizon, or extend our present one if we are to discover and know something new, or something more than the old. The new itself can appear in the garments of the old, just as the old can deceive us by a semblance of the new, for we see only the surface, and this surface we often see darkly and through a mist. It is God alone who can produce the new, disclose it to us, and teach us to distinguish and discern it. God explicitly ascribes all this to himself in Holy Scripture. Ecclesiastes seems to have been chiefly written in order that he, the wisest of all seekers after wisdom, might point to the revelation of God in the flesh and the preaching of his kingdom as the sole new thing that would be significantly, universally and really new for all the earth and would never cease to be new. God therefore caused a rumour of this new thing to spread through the earth before-hand . . . Jesus the crucified is the only subject for which the instinct of curiosity has been implanted in us by God, the only subject which can satisfy this instinct, and which transforms our curiosity into wisdom. This is a thirst we feel despite our original sin, a thirst increased by every earthly fountain, which heightens the fever instead of beating it down, quenching it. It is a craving which every outward satisfaction and earthly medicine makes more perilous, and burning, and widespread; which cries for the balm of Gilead to produce not palliation and healing but joy and refreshment of a quite opposite kind. The thirst that cries for palliation is that of a sick man which is only made worse by the drink he receives. But this thirst is that of a tired and parched man who has a pure spring, a cooling and refreshing nectar, to revive him. For the more he drinks the richer the stream, and it is impossible to drink too much, for our thirst is maintained by the sweetness and richness, the very effect, of this stream.

This is one of the countless contradictions in our nature which we cannot solve. Reason is inclined to serve an unknown God, but is infinitely remote from knowing him. It does not wish to know him—and what is even more astonishing, when it does know him it ceases to serve him. This is why God discloses himself so late and so slowly, for he knows that the knowledge of him is a stumbling-block and an offence to man, that he is foolishness and a thorn in the flesh to him as soon as he wishes to reveal himself and make himself known to him. When Jesus said that he was the Son of God, thus disclosing the most comforting, important and new truth, the Jews lifted stones, rent their garments, and condemned him as a malefactor. The Athenians were devoutly ready to fall down before an unknown God; but immediately this unknown God was disclosed to them, they cared no more: they mocked and thought they were hearing, not something new, but matters of indifference, not worth investigating and knowing in their context, or receiving fresh insight about.

II Thessalonians 2

God repeats himself, in nature as in Scripture, in the government of the world, in the building up of his church, in the course of the ages—at least it seems so to us, and it is necessary for us that we see repetition. It is not the same fruits, yet it is the same, which every spring produces; it is not the same body, yet it is the same, which comes from our mother's womb and which we sow in the womb of the earth; it is not the same river, yet it is the same, which seems to swallow itself. He who can explain a speck of dust in the sun's rays possesses the secret of all nature. And the spirit, which explores the depths of the godhead, puts a mysterious word in Samson's mouth which a trivial event makes comprehensible, a word whose meaning is revealed by that same mystery of which Paul was an apostle and which he calls his gospel (Romans 16. 25-6).

Hebrews 11. 3

Without faith we cannot understand even creation and nature— hence the efforts to set God's Word and Will at a distance, to explain existence by means of hypotheses and probabilities;

hence the many doubts that have been raised about the story of Moses.

Revelation 1. 4

How imperfect and inadequate men's ideas are to represent heavenly and spiritual things! God's eternity can only be grasped through the divisions of time, through a combination of three moments which in our inadequacy we are forced to compare and distinguish. The unchangeableness of God, in which, as James says (1. 17), there is no variation or shadow due to change, can only be made clear to us by means of the changing nature of earthly things. In our conceptions the past precedes the present; with God the present is the ground of the past and the future. What can give us a more wonderful and mysterious idea of God's unchanging and inexhaustible greatness and unfathomable heights than this destruction, or this surpassing, of all human ideas! In this Name of God there is not only an image of the Holy Trinity, but also in particular of our divine Redeemer. He is— I am with you always, till the close of the age—he was—the Word became flesh and dwelt among us, full of grace and truth—he will be—Behold, I come, is written of me in the book. Come, Lord Jesus!

THOUGHTS ABOUT MY LIFE

1758

Written in London, under great stress, directly after the
turning-point in his life, with the date 21 April, 1758, this
autobiographical sketch bears marks of the pietist background of Hamann's upbringing, but goes beyond even its
own style in the depth of its passions and the vigour of its
thought. The introductory sections, on his early life in
Königsberg, and as a house tutor in Livonia and Courland,
some concluding reflections, added later, and a few other
passages, are omitted. The main bulk of the
story is translated here.

THOUGHTS ABOUT MY LIFE

WHILE I wandered in the forecourts of knowledge I lost the vocation I had thought I had for Divinity. I found an obstacle in my speech, in my poor memory, and many hypocritical obstacles in my way of thinking, in the corrupt morals of the clerical profession and in the importance I set on its duties. I was certainly right, so long as I considered myself as the giver and author of what belongs to that profession. I forgot the source of all good, from which I could expect and promise myself all that I lacked, and with whose support I could have overcome all that lay in my way . . .

What took away my taste for theology and all serious learning was a new inclination that had arisen in me for antiquities and criticism, and thence for so-called *belles lettres*, poetry, novels, philology, the French writers with their poetic gift of description and depiction, of pleasing the imagination, and so on. God, my gracious God, hear and forgive me the misuse of my natural powers, which by a proper use might have been capable of preeminent distinction and profit for the world as well as for myself, powers which I had in fact dedicated to the service of his house and his work on earth, powers which I have so mutilated and corrupted—forgive the waste of precious time, my father's expenses, his hope to have in his children a support for his old age. Correct what I have corrupted, if it is not too late, and bless the more the time of grace which thou wilt still vouchsafe me. Let all my errors be for my good, and let them enable me at last to become wise, and with all the more emphasis and zeal warn others off the cliffs on which I myself was wrecked.

I gave myself out, therefore, to be a student of law. In my folly I saw a kind of high-spiritedness and loftiness in not studying for a living but according to inclination, to while away the time, and for love of knowledge itself. I thought it was better to be a martyr than a day-labourer and hireling of the muses. What nonsense can be expressed in rounded and high-sounding words! So I heard lectures on the *Institutions* and the *Pandects* without preparation or revision, without seriousness or any real intention of becoming a lawyer, just as I had neither had nor shown any to be a theologian.

Meanwhile it had always been in my mind to obtain a post as house tutor, in order that I might have an opportunity, and try out my freedom in the world. My dear parents' house seemed to me to exercise a compulsion at some points, and I wanted to be master of my money, of which for my good I was partly kept a little too short, and partly learned too late, when I had my own, to make better use. Perhaps there was also no divine blessing on what I earned; for the divine blessing makes even a little superfluous. Disorder, the general and basic defect of my character, a false generosity, a love that was too blind in welcoming the judgments of others, and a carelessness that sprang partly from inexperience and ignorance—these were all at fault in my life. . . . I left my parents' house in November 1752, when my dear mother broke down with sadness, and my father accompanied me to the gate of the town. . . . I arrived at Papendorf, the parish of the estate, on a Saturday, and on the Sunday I saw the family in whose home I was to belong: a child of nine, who looked very modest, awkward and delicate, and his young sister and an orphan girl whom the baroness was bringing up. The beginning I made in this new calling was certainly difficult. I had to educate myself, my young pupil, and an uncouth, rough and ignorant mother. I went like a spirited horse in the plough, with great zeal, honest intentions, little sense, and too much trust in myself and confidence in human follies for the good that I did or wanted to do. We are naturally inclined to overestimate our own efforts, to look for their results as an inevitable consequence, to weigh and calculate the duties of others according to our own prejudices and inclinations. The farmer cannot promise himself hundred-fold fruits from the careful art of husbandry alone. The earth, the weather, the quality of the seed, the presence of vermin, things that escape our notice, have their share, and over everything there is the blessing of divine providence and governance. I wanted my actions to be recognised by men, at times admired; I even wanted to put men to shame. These are all disingenuous impulses, which dissipate and ruin the use of our powers. God bestowed on me infinite grace, he gave me more patience than I was capable of, more cleverness, more happiness, all of which I may have ascribed to myself, and which may have been the effect of the prayer of my pious parents and the forbearance of his divine long-suffering and grace. My unsociable or peculiar way of living, which was partly a pose, partly false cleverness, partly a consequence of an inner unrest with which I had been afflicted for a very long time; dissatisfaction and inability to endure my own self, and the vanity to make oneself an enigma—everything combined to spoil much and to make me offensive. I wrote two letters to the baroness about the upbringing of her child, which were meant to awaken her conscience. They were not understood, and the receiving of them poured oil on the fire. I was therefore unexpectedly dismissed, without having been six months in the house, with some humbling of my pride. But I had some satisfaction in the affection of the child, and the flattering thought of innocence, or of being repaid evil for good. I wrapped myself so far as I could in the mantle of religion and virtue, in order to cover my nakedness; but I stormed with rage to revenge and justify myself. This was a folly which I myself perceived with the passage of time, and which therefore evaporated.

Thereafter I spent some months in Riga, used up the little money I had received, and was besides in debt to my landlord, who was the same compatriot of my father's with whom I had stayed on my arrival. This time was divided between a wild misanthropic industry and excesses of pleasure and idleness. My money melted away to the last ducat, which I had the folly to spend on some useless books. I had lived heedlessly, making only a few vain attempts to obtain a new post. God took pity on me, and made use of the brother-in-law of the baroness to open for me the very advantageous opportunity of a door into Courland, when I was on the brink of extreme want, and had already on that account passed many sleepless nights . . .

I arrived when the people of Riga were enjoying life at their country houses, and had the good fortune to take the Pyrmont waters with the Berens family. My health had suffered severely, partly through teaching, partly through disorderly attention to secondary matters, and partly through the tumult of emotions in which my spirit was continually driven hither and thither like a frail craft on a stormy sea. This beneficial opportunity came therefore very fittingly. In spite of every cause for satisfaction I could not yield to joy in the company of the noblest, gayest, best-hearted men and women. My brain saw a mist of ideas around it which it could not distinguish. My heart felt stirrings which I could not explain. I felt nothing but suspicion of myself and others, nothing but torment about how I should draw near them or disclose myself to them; and in this condition I lived for the most part in that house where I was the most fervent admirer, worshipper and friend of all who belonged to it. How is it possible that I could have been taken for a clever, not to say a serviceable man, when I have never been able to discover what I am and can be? This is a mystery I have never been able to understand or clarify. That is why I look on all these things partly as presentiments and partly as effects of the hand of God, which lay heavy upon me, so that amid all the good done to me by men I should not recognise myself. I regard all the unrest in which I lived as a consequence of that, and I console myself that God will now throw away this rod under which I sighed without recognising it, and will disclose to me his gracious will, to which I am completely surrendered. I have been a premature fruit in all my deeds and actions, in all my undertakings and projects, because they have been dared and begun without God, and have come to nothing, instead of reaching a proper conclusion. In the end I kicked till I was wounded and bloody against the pricks that I did not want to recognise, and pray only that the gracious God who according to his promise forgives the repentant and believing sinner and forgets all that is past will make my future life new and holy . . .

My time in Amsterdam was just as lost. I was in confusion and did not know whether to turn to business or to learning. I had lost all my luck in finding friends and acquaintances of my own class and disposition—a matter I had hitherto been very proud of. I thought that everyone shunned me, and I myself shunned everyone. I can offer no reason for it except that God's hand was heavy upon me, that I had set him out of my sight and forsaken him, and confessed and besought him with a lukewarm heart and with my lips alone, that my ways did not please him, that in spite of his remembering me and stirring my heart I did not want to recognise my guilt, that I sought ever more distraction, but in vain, that finally I would almost have denied my taste in order to escape from myself. And in the greatest part of my life I find this reason to be the stumbling-block, which has led me to misuse and mock and slander all the good that God has vouchsafed me. So I set out to make my fortune. I always carried about with me the self-reproach that in whatever the change I had now made I had not acted well. I therefore had to use it merely as a means to snatch a better opportunity for attaining my fortune, and I would have done this if I had found an opportunity which put me in the position to satisfy my friends. All in vain: no man was able to know me; no man wanted to know me. I had to run my course to the end, and see the goal of my heedless desires, my foolish inclinations, my extravagant conceits.

Finally I got my wish to go to England, accompanied by the most pressing generosity. My last destination yielded me my only and last hope. I was supported in my hope by a ridiculous partiality for that land, which I had always looked upon as the home or proper base and place for my adventurer's way of living and thinking. I left Amsterdam by a canal-boat on Maundy Thursday or Good Friday, which I considered it unnecessary to observe, since in England and Holland it is not regarded as a festival, and I celebrated Easter at Leyden in the greatest disorder and oppression of spirit. Thereafter I went to Rotterdam, where I stayed at Swienshofd, the best inn, and there found a young Englishman seeking company, with whom I had travelled from Amsterdam to Leyden. This suited me very well, and I was already painting flattering pictures of my acquaintance with him, which came to a bad end. We chartered a yacht for Helvoetsluys, where on the same day, 16 April, a Saturday, the packet-boat left . . . and arrived with a fair wind at Harwich on the Sunday evening . . .

We arrived late in the evening of 18 April, 1757, in London. There I spent a very restless night with my Bremen acquaintance at the inn, for it seemed to be a den of murderers, full of a perfect rabble; our room was so insecure that anyone could get in by the window who did not want to waken us by coming in by the door. In London every window can be opened by pushing it up.

I had a few days' breathing-space before I saw to my business, and found a good inn along with my Bremen friend, who was accompanied by a guide and friend, a young merchant engaged to his sister. After I had engaged a lackey came my first folly: I sought out a quack of whom I had heard that he could cure every impediment of speech. He lives in Islington. I inquired about him at a German inn where he was very well known, and I was told that he had performed some cures which had made him famous. But they could see no reason for my need of him. I went to him, and found an old man who examined me and could see nothing wrong with my organs of speech, and made it a condition of his curing me that I stay in his house and pay him a large sum of money: for a certain time I was not to speak at all, and then I was to learn to spell out words. I could not extract any more from him about his method. So I had to set about my business with the same old tongue and the same old heart. I revealed the nature of my business to those to whom I had been directed. They were astonished at its importance, even more at the way it was conducted, and perhaps most of all at the person to whom these matters had been entrusted. After they had recovered from their first wonderment they began to smile—impudently disclosing their thoughts—at those who had sent me, at the reason for my coming, and commiserated with me. All these things unsettled me, and at the same time enraged me. Finally I worked at a memorial to the Russian ambassador—that was all I could do. He took away all hope from me that anything could be done, and gave me all the more assurance of his zeal to serve me, that the latter might perhaps be reckoned in his favour if the former were realised. There are certain posts and affairs which may be best and most honourably managed if nothing or as little as possible is done. If we were to make a point of taking heed of everything possible, then we would first have to set aside our comfort and peace, then expose ourselves to great danger and responsibility, perhaps make enemies, and be sacrificed to our good will and impotence. In these circumstances is a minister who regards treason to his duties, and to the honour of him whom he represents, and so on, as cleverness and foresight, who oppresses the interest of others for the sake of his own security, who regards difficulties as impossibilities. So I believed that I had to manage my business in accordance with precisely these rules, and do as little as possible in order not to heap up expenses, and through over-hasty steps expose myself to attack and discredit; and that I had to regard this little as all that was convenient and practicable. So with oppressed and reeling spirit I went hither and thither, and had no one to whom I could unbosom myself and who could advise and help me.

I was near despair, and tried to hold it off and suppress it by sheer distractions. What was blindness and madness and indeed wickedness appeared to me as the only means of salvation. Let the world go as it will—with the blasphemy of a confidence in providence which helps in a wonderful way—take everything along with you that you chance upon, in order to forget yourself —this was the system on which I wished to model my conduct, and which collapsed with every unlucky effort, but which I again built up with the same end in view. My main proposition was simply an opportunity—a good opportunity. God knows what I would not have regarded as an opportunity to pay my debts and be able to enter unburdened on a new folly.

So I gave up everything; the vain efforts aroused by the letters and representations of appreciative friends were mere semblance, rotten wood, wills-o'-the-wisp born of the bog. My good humour and my heroic spirit were nothing but the chimera of a knight errant and the bells of my fool's cap.

In Berlin I had been foolish enough to take lessons on the lute for a week from the lutenist, Baron; my upright father admonished and punished me for it, I had to think of my profession and my eyes. This had been in vain. Satan tempted me again with the lute, which had caused me trouble in Berlin, for I had in my ignorance spoiled one which I had borrowed from a poor student called Viermetz who lived by his music, and had not compensated him for it, but had rather felt insulted by his modest and touching sensitivity. Thus I began again to inquire for a lute, as though my whole happiness depended on this instrument in which I possess so little ability. It was not possible to find one, and I was told there was not more than a single lutenist in London, who could have earned a great deal but now lived like a lord. I was afire to get to know him, and had my wish. How severely I was punished through this man! He became my confidant, I went daily in and out, and came to stay nearby; he had his own house, and kept a mistress. He offered me everything; however distant my first judgment of him had kept me from him, however many scruples I had about his character, he had an explanation for everything. I thought I had now found what I wanted: you can become known through him, now you have at least one man with whom you can associate, you have a house where you can find distraction, you can practise the lute and step into his place, you can become as fortunate as he. ——I thank God that he loved me better than that, and that he freed me from a man to whom I had joined myself like a mill-slave in order to walk with him the same way of sin and vice.

My blind heart made me see good intentions in my association with him—to instil taste and principles into a man without them and without education. Blind as I was, I wanted to lead another, or perhaps instruct him to sin elegantly, to turn reason into wickedness. In vain I gorged, in vain I drank and whored and rushed about. In vain I rang the changes on debauchery and reflection, reading and knavery, industry and voluptuous idleness: in vain I ran to excess in both. In nine months I changed my lodgings almost monthly, nowhere did I find rest, everywhere I found deceitful, base, avaricious people.

The last straw was the unmasking of my friend, who had already supplied me with an infinite number of marks of suspicion, which I suppressed. I learned that he was maintained in a shameful way by a rich Englishman. Known by the name of Senel, he gave himself out to be a German Baron von Pournoaille, and had a sister in London probably maintained in a similar way by the Russian ambassador, bearing a son under the name of Frau von Perl. I was horrified at this rumour and wanted to be certain. A long time before, he had entrusted me with a packet of letters, which despite their alleged importance he had forgotten to ask for, and which I too, from I know not what presentiment, had not returned, without its ever having occurred to me to abuse his confidence. They were very loosely sealed. I could not now resist the temptation to obtain certainty from them. So I broke the seal, and made the excuse to myself that if I found nothing in them about the crime attributed to him I would return them to him with the forthright confession of my meddlesomeness, and swear all possible secrecy to him about the rest. But at the same time I would repudiate my friendship with him in so far as I discovered other secrets which went against my principles. Unfortunately I found too much which convinced me of his infamy. They were abominable and ridiculous love-letters in a hand that I knew was that of his alleged good friend.

I was very restless about the measures I had to take, but in my cunning I thought I had to withhold some of the letters which contained the greatest proofs of his crime, and to leave the use of them to time and circumstance. He had spent some time in the country with the companion and employer of his wickedness. When he returned he asked with great circumspection for his letters, which I handed to him with some disturbance and which he received with even more. I wanted to open my mind to him and make my representations about the matter. So I accepted being on the old footing with him, though without the heart for it. It appeared that he had merely wanted to spare me, in order to discover whether I knew something of the secret of wickedness. As I had apparently set him at ease about the matter, he thought that he had a perfect right to cut himself off gradually from me. I forestalled him, and had made another resolution—to write myself to the Englishman, whom I knew, in order to put before him the ignominy and peril of his association with his companion in wickedness. I did this with as much emphasis as I was capable of, but failed to achieve my aim: instead of separating, they joined forces to stop my mouth.

Meanwhile I had moved to a coffee-house, since I had not a soul to consort with, in order to seek some cheer in society, and by this means perhaps to become known and build a bridge to fortune. This was always the first aim of all I did. It was too expensive and too full of temptations for me to stay. I was reduced to a few guineas, and had to move again. Full of fear and care I went out to find another room. God was so gracious as to let me find one with very honest and good people, the Collinses in Marlborough Street, where I have been since 8 February of this year, 1758. They are young people, who make it a point of honour to let everyone know that they have been servants and have started a little business which God has visibly blessed, and they recognise this with gratitude, unflagging industry, and humility. It is a special favour of providence to have let me find this house in which I live in the most inexpensive and contented way, since I need not fear to be overcharged by a single heller, and enjoy the best attention free of charge. I have wondered why God did not let me find this house earlier, which would have been able to save me sooner. He alone knows the time, the best time to show us the beginning of his help. We, who deserve nothing but wrath and the misfortune for which we strive, expostulate with God why he will not help us sooner, us who do not want to be helped.

In that coffee-house I had suffered from constipation for a week at a time, and been astonishingly and insatiably hungry. I had poured strong English beer into myself like water. Thus my good health during all the disorder of my way of life and of my spirit is a divine miracle—as indeed without a doubt is my life itself and its preservation. In this house, though I have been almost three months here now, I have not had a proper meal more than four times. My whole nourishment is gruel, with coffee once a day. God has caused this nourishment to flourish extraordinarily, and I mean with his help to hold out as long as possible with it. The most powerful reason for this diet has been need, yet it is perhaps the only means of restoring my body from the consequences of excess.

I have gone through £150 here, and can and will go no further. My debts in Livonia and Courland therefore amount to over £300 . . . I have no more money, and have given my landlord my watch. The company of the aforementioned fellow has cost me much useless expenditure. My frequent change of lodgings has likewise cost me much. I have bought two suits of clothes, the waistcoat of one pretty richly bedecked, and a mass of books. In this house I wanted to cut myself off from all society, and seek to console myself with nothing but my books, of which a fair number are still unread or at least read profitlessly without reflection and proper application. God had inspired me at the same time to procure a bible, which I sought with great ardour till I found one I liked, and of which till now I have been a very indifferent owner. My isolation, the prospect of complete penury and beggary—for which at times in despair I had striven, looking on that condition as a means of encouraging me to a bold stroke of fortune—I even wished for poverty with a more wicked intention, in order to tempt anew and deliberately, with sinful audacity, the gracious God of my life, who had always stood by me in the extreme of my need: in short, the aridity of my circumstances and the depth of my affliction took from me the taste for my books. They were poor comforters to me, those friends whom I did not think I could do without, for whose company I had had such a longing that I looked on them as the only support and ornament of human destiny.

In the tumult of the passions which overwhelmed me, so that often I could not find breath, I continually prayed to God for a friend, for a wise and upright friend, such as I could no longer picture to myself. Instead I had tasted, tasted enough, the gall of false friendship and the inaccessibility of any betterment. A friend who could supply the key to my heart, the clue to lead me out of my labyrinth, was a wish I often had, without properly understanding or seeing its content. Praise God, I found this friend in my heart, who crept in there at the time when I felt most keenly its emptiness and darkness and wilderness. In that time, if I am not mistaken, I had read the Old Testament once through and the New Testament twice. I wanted to make a fresh start with it, and it seemed as if I were conscious of a blanket over my mind and my heart, which had sealed this book from me the first time. So I planned to read it with more attention and in better order, and with a greater hunger, and to set down the thoughts that came to me.

This beginning, when I still brought to my reading very imperfect and impure thoughts about God's Word, was nevertheless made with more honesty than formerly, on 13 March. The farther I went, the newer it became to me, the more divine did I perceive its content and effect to be. I forgot all my other books, I was ashamed ever to have compared them with the book of God, ever to have set them side by side, ever to have preferred another book to it. I found the unity of the divine will in the redemption of Jesus Christ, so that all history, all miracles, all commands and works of God flowed towards this centre, to stir the soul of man from the slavery, bondage, blindness, folly and death of sins to the greatest happiness, the highest blessedness and an acceptance of goods whose greatness, when revealed to us, must terrify us more than our own unworthiness or the possibility of making ourselves worthy of them. I recognised my own crimes in the history of the Jewish people, I read the course of my own life and thanked God for his longsuffering with this his people, since nothing but such an example could justify me in a like hope. Above all I found in the books of the Law a remarkable disclosure, that the Israelites, however crude they appear to us, nevertheless in some cases sought from God nothing but what he was willing to do for them; that they acknowledged their disobedience in as lively a way as any repentant sinner ever did, and forgot their penitence just as quickly; but that in their fear they called for nothing else but a Redeemer, an Advocate, a Mediator, without whom they could neither fear nor love God aright. With these reflections, which seemed to me very mysterious, in the evening of 31 March I read the fifth chapter of Deuteronomy, and fell into deep thought. I thought of Abel of whom God said, The earth has opened her mouth to receive thy brother's blood.—I felt my heart thump, I heard a voice sigh in its depths and wail like the voice of blood, like the voice of a slain brother who wanted to avenge his blood if I did not hear it betimes and went on stopping my ears to it, saying that it was just this which made Cain a wanderer and a fugitive. All at once I felt my heart swell, and pour out in tears, and I could no longer —I could no longer conceal from my God that I was the fratricide, the murderer of his only begotten Son. The Spirit of God went on, in spite of great weakness, and the long resistance I had made against his witness and his stirring of me, to reveal to me more and more the mystery of the divine love and the benefit of faith in our gracious and only Saviour.

153

With sighs that were brought before God by an Interpreter who is beloved and dear to him, I went on with the reading of the divine Word, and enjoyed that very help with which it was written as the only way to understand it, and with the divine aid I brought my work to an unbroken conclusion, on 21 April, with extraordinarily rich consolation and quickening.

Now, thank God, I feel my heart more at rest than ever before in my life. At the times when melancholy has begun to arise I have been overwhelmed with a consolation the source of which I cannot ascribe to myself, and which no man can instil so inexhaustibly into his neighbour. I have been frightened by its excess. It swallowed up all fear, all sadness, all mistrust, so that I could no longer find a trace of them in my spirit. I pray God he will bless the work he has begun in me, strengthening my weak faith by his Word and the Spirit, the gracious abundant Spirit of the Word, the Spirit of peace which passes all understanding and is not such a peace as the world gives, the Spirit of love, without which we are nothing but enemies of God (and he who hates this Benefactor, how can he love in temporal things?), and the Spirit of hope that does not make ashamed like the shadow-play of worldly illusions.

Since I have received from God the great good, the priceless pearl, the prize for which he brought me into life, how should I now doubt his government of my whole life? Its end is reached. I surrender myself to his wise and alone good will. I know now the blindness and corruption of my own will too well not to relinquish it. My sins are debts of infinitely more importance and consequence than my temporal debts. The gaining of the whole world would not be able to pay for my sins; and if Abraham had to hear from Ephron, a Canaanite, on account of 400 shekels of silver, these words, What is that between me and thee? should not God make a Christian, if he is set right in the highest matter of all, think more magnanimous thoughts than a heathen?

What should it matter to God to throw a little thing in addition into the transaction? The £300 are his debt; he will deal with me as Paul did with Philemon's slave, and will know how to settle it in accordance with his wisdom.

I have set down these thoughts about my life for myself or my dear father and brother, and wish that they may be worth reading by them or my closest friends. In them I have spoken with God and myself. I have justified God with regard to my life, and I have accused myself, denounced and uncovered myself —all to the praise of the alone good God, who has forgiven me in the blood of his only begotten Son and in the witness that the Spirit of God confirms in his Word and in my heart. God has poured me from one vessel to the other lest I get soured and foul beyond redemption. Everything must serve for our good; since the death of sin brings life to us, so all its sicknesses must make for the experience, the illustration and the glory of God. He who compares the map of Israel's wanderings with the course of my own life will see how accurately they correspond. I believe that the end of my pilgrimage will lead me by the grace of God into the promised land—supposing that I should not have the time and opportunity here to make amends for the disorder and the damage that I have brought on others. My friends would of course be more grieved if I died of the poison of sorrow and despair. My good health and my life, I repeat, are at once a miracle and a sign that God did not despair of my recovery nor of my future usefulness for his service. My son, give me thy heart!—Here it is, my God! Thou hast demanded it, blind, hard, flinty, astray, unrepentant though it was. Purify it, make it new, and let it be the workshop of thy good Spirit. It has deceived me so often when it was in my hands that I no longer wish to acknowledge it as mine. It is a leviathan that thou alone canst tame—through thy indwelling it will enjoy rest and comfort and blessedness.

I close with a proof of my own experience, in hearty and up-right thanks to God for his blessed Word which I have tested and found to be the only light, not only to come to God but also to know ourselves; to be the most precious gift of divine grace that exceeds all nature and all its treasures as much as our immortal spirit exceeds the clay of flesh and blood; to be the most amazing and adorable revelation of the deepest, loftiest, most wonderful secrets of the godhead in heaven, on earth, and in hell, secrets of God's nature, attributes, and great and abundant will especially towards us wretched men, full of the most important disclosures through the course of all ages into eternity; to be the only bread and manna for our souls, which a Christian can less easily do without than the earthly man can do without his daily needs and sustenance—yes: I confess that this Word of God performs just as great miracles in the soul of a pious Christian, be he simple or learned, as the miracles that are recorded in it; that therefore the understanding of this book and faith in its contents is to be attained only through the very same Spirit who impelled its authors; that its sighs that cannot be uttered, which he creates in our hearts, are of the same nature as the inexpressible images which are poured forth in Holy Scripture with a greater richness than all the seeds of all nature and its realms.

Secondly, there is the confession of my heart and my best reason that it is impossible without faith in Jesus Christ to know God, his loving, inexpressibly good and beneficent being, whose wisdom, omnipotence and all other attributes seem to be only, as it were, instruments of his love for men; that this preferring of men, these insects of creation, is part of the greatest depths of the divine revelation; that Jesus Christ was not only content to have become a man, but a poor man, the most wretched of men; that the Holy Spirit set forth for us a book for his Word, wherein like a fool and a madman, like an unholy and impure spirit, he made for our proud reason childish stories and contemptible events into the history of heaven and God (I Cor. 1. 25)—that this faith reveals all our own actions and the noblest fruits of human virtue to us as nothing but the sketches of the finest pen, or the tenderest skin, seen under a magnifying-glass; that it is therefore impossible without faith in God, which is created by his Spirit and the work of the only Mediator, to love ourselves and our neighbour; in short, a man must be a true Christian in order to be a proper father, a proper child, a good citizen, a true patriot, a good subject, a good master and a good servant; and that every good, in the strictest sense of the word, is impossible without God, that he is indeed the only author of good.

FRAGMENTS

1758

These reflections, a *parergon* of the London
experience, are translated in full.

FRAGMENTS

Gather up the fragments left over, that
nothing may be lost.

JOHN 6. 12

LONDON, 16 MAY, 1758

Explanation of the Title

A GREAT company of people was fed by five barley loaves, and much was left over. This little amount was so plentiful for the multitude in the wilderness that more full baskets were left over than the number of loaves they had received. We see the same miracle of the divine blessing in the abundance of the sciences and arts. What a storehouse the history of learning is! And what is the basis of it all? Five barley loaves, the five senses which we have in common with the brute creation. Not only the whole warehouse of reason, but also the treasure-house of faith itself, rest on this basis. Our reason is like that blind Theban soothsayer Tiresias, to whom his daughter Manto described the flight of the birds, and he prophesied from her accounts. Faith, says the apostle, comes by hearing, by hearing the Word of God (Romans 10. 17). Go, and tell John what you hear and see (Matthew 11. 4).

Man enjoys infinitely more than he needs—and destroys infinitely more than he enjoys. How wasteful nature must be for the sake of her children; how condescending in balancing our numbers and our needs, and in spending herself to satisfy the hunger and the insolence of our desires. Must she not be the daughter of a very loving father and friend of man?

160

How much more does man sin, in his complaints about the prison of the body, the restrictions placed upon him by his senses, and the imperfection of his light, when at the same time he condemns his senses by his insatiable lusts of the flesh, by his partiality for sensual prejudices, and by his pride in the very light which he belittles. However much the visible world is a wilderness in the eyes of a spirit created for heaven, however mean and meagre the loaves may look which God serves us here, however small the fish, they are blessed—and we with them—by an almighty, wonder-working and mysterious God, whom we Christians call our God because he has revealed himself as such in the greatest humility and love.

Does not our spirit itself, in the depths of its misery, betray this sign of its high origin, when it rises as a creator above sense-impressions, making them fruitful, and building them into a scaffolding to climb to heaven; or when it creates idols for itself for which it burns bricks and gathers stubble? Is it not a miracle of our spirit that it transforms the poverty of the senses into such richness and astonishing expansion?

Our soul is just as guilty of dissipation in the nourishment of its powers as it is in its dissipation in the body. Apart from the moderation which our needy state should prescribe for us, we should not reprove an economic attention to the fragments we let fall in the heat of our appetites, which we do not think worth collecting because we see more before us. Here on earth we live on fragments. Our thoughts are fragments. Our knowledge itself is patchwork. With God's help I mean to make up a basket of such thoughts, in which I will gather up the fruits of my reading and reflection in scattered and varied thoughts. In order that in due course I may bring together those of like content, I will number them.

I

Do we not use the concept of freedom to describe what are mere manifestations of self-love? This self-love is the heart of our will, from which all inclinations and desires flow like our arteries and veins. We can no more think than we can will, without being conscious of our self.

The Japanese sees his idol as closely connected with his ideas and inclinations as the Russian his beard and the Englishman his Magna Carta. The superstitious man, the slave and the republican struggle with a like fury and desert for the object of their self-love, and with the same basis of freedom and zeal.

Why does trade increase the love of freedom? Because it increases the property of a people as well as that of every citizen. We love what is our own. Freedom is therefore nothing but one's own profit, and a branch of self-love directed towards our own goods.

That is why the effects of self-love and freedom bear so many resemblances to one another. Self-love indeed governs freedom, as Young says:

> man love thyself;
> In this alone free-agents are not free.

Just as all our powers of knowledge have self-knowledge for their object, so self-love is the object of our inclinations and desires. Self-knowledge is our wisdom, self-love our virtue. It is impossible for a man to love himself so long as he is unable to know himself. Hence the truth alone can make us free; this is the teaching of the heavenly wisdom which came into the world in order to teach us self-knowledge and self-love.

Why cannot man know his own self? The reason must lie simply in the condition of our souls. Nature, which instructs us about the invisible world in sheer riddles and parables, shows us by means of the relations on which our body depends how we are to understand the relation of our spirit to other spirits. Just as the body is subject to the laws of external objects, air, earth, and the influence of other bodies, so we must understand our soul. It is exposed to the constant influence of higher spirits, and is bound up with them. This is what undoubtedly makes our own self so ambiguous that we cannot recognise, distinguish or define it.

The impossibility of knowing our own self can lie in the basis of our nature as well as in its particular constitution and condition. The movement of a clock presupposes both a proper construction and its being wound. If our nature depends in a special and precise manner upon the will of a higher being, then it follows that we must make use of the concept of such a being in order to explain human nature; and that the more light we receive in contemplating this being, the more must our own nature be illuminated.

Our life is the first of all goods, and the source of happiness. If we consider our life in this way, then its constitution will throw light on the qualities of happiness. Happiness is so dependent that countless accidents can rob us of it, and we have no more power over it than every external thing can boast. The mass of hostile causes that can break the bond of soul and body is nevertheless governed by him to whom we owe our life. All the mediating instruments are in his hands. Hence the same is true of our happiness. Thus we may see that our self is so necessarily grounded in the Creator that we do not have the knowledge of our self in our own power, and that, in order to measure its extent, we must penetrate to the bosom of the godhead, who alone can determine and resolve the whole mystery of our being.

It is therefore unavoidable that we summon the help of the

first cause of all things, on which we are so directly dependent, if we wish to understand our own self, our nature, our destiny and limitations. Next to this first cause we need a knowledge of all the intermediary beings with which we are bound together, whose influence is able to produce or to change our own. All these reflections, taken together, may be described as the condition of human nature in the world. In order to fathom my own self it is not enough to know what man is, but also what his condition is. Are you free, or a slave? Are you under age, an orphan, or a widow, and in what way are you regarded by the higher beings who take it upon themselves to manage you, who oppress you, take advantage of you, and seek to profit by your ignorance and weakness and folly?

We may see from this on how many factors our self-knowledge rests, and how impossible or inadequate or deceptive it is, so long as these factors are not disclosed to us. So the reason can only conceive analogies, which give it a very uncertain light; and our observations of the plan of the divine creation and governance can only yield us suppositions about the particular form of his secret will with us.

Our life consists of a union of the visible part with a higher being whom we can infer only from his effects. This union is to some extent in the power of our own will—and exposed to countless other hazards. Both the visible and the invisible part of our life are, in an incomprehensible and hidden way, under the governance and providence of him who gives us life and preserves it in accordance with his will. These and similar ideas are indicators to which we must pay heed in order to reach conclusions about our self.

In order to make easier the knowledge of our self, my own self is visible as in a mirror in every neighbour. As the image of my face is reflected in water, so my I is reflected in every neighbour. That this I may be as dear to me as my own, providence has sought to unite as many advantages and amenities in human society as possible.

God and my neighbour are therefore a part of my self-knowledge, my self-love. What a law, what a delightful law-giver, who commands us to love himself with all our heart, and our neighbour as our self! This is the true and only human self-love, the supreme wisdom of a Christian's self-knowledge, who not only loves God as the supreme, most beneficent, alone good and perfect being, but also knows that this God has in the strictest sense become his and his fellow-man's neighbour, in order that we might have every possible reason for loving God and our neighbour.

So we see that in our faith alone are heavenly knowledge, true happiness and the loftiest freedom of human nature united. Reason, spirit, and morality are three daughters of a true doctrine of nature, which has no better source than revelation.

2

How frightened we should be by the greatness of our nature, when we consider that the choice not only of the good, but of the best, is a law of our will. The structure of every creature is related to its destiny. Is not this calling prophetic of supreme happiness?

3

According to Roman law no soldier was allowed to buy land in the country where he was waging war.[1] This Roman law condemns the Christian, who is called to be a warrior on this earth, who tries to settle down in this world. In the histories,

[1] The references given in Roth and in Nadler differ, but are alike incomprehensible. Hamann intended to refer his readers to *Digest*, xlix, 16, 9 and 13. I owe this reference to Professor C. J. Fordyce.

laws and customs of all nations we find what we may term the *sensum communem* of religion. Everything lives and is full of hints of our calling and of the God of grace. We are very prejudiced if we limit God's effects and influence merely to the Jewish people. In the example of that people he has merely declared and made available to our senses the hiddenness, the method and the laws of his wisdom and love, and has left to us the application of this to our own life and to other objects, peoples and events. The Apostle says explicitly to the people of Lystra that God has not left the heathen without a witness of himself; and in what did this consist? He did good to them, he made himself known to them as love and as the God of love, he gave them rain from heaven and fruitful seasons and filled their hearts with food and joy (Acts 14. 17). Here it is clearly seen that the rain and the fruitful seasons are not just weather, but show the effects of the spirit, imparting to us good thoughts, good tendencies and good designs, which is ascribed to the Jews in such a distinctive manner that it is even said of their women that they needed the spirit's help to spin wool for the tabernacle.

If the tiniest blade of grass is a proof of God, why should the tiniest actions of man have less significance? Did Scripture not seek out this most despicable of people, one of the smallest, and its worst, even its most sinful actions, in order to clothe God's providence and wisdom and to reveal him in this lowliness of images? Nature and history are therefore the two great commentaries on the divine Word, and this Word is the only key to unlock a knowledge of both. What does the difference between natural and revealed knowledge mean? If I understand it aright, the difference is no more than that between the eye of a man who sees a picture without understanding the least thing about painting or drawing or the story that is represented, and the eye of a painter; or between natural hearing and a musical ear.

Might one not say of Socrates, when he spoke of his guardian spirit, what is written of Peter: "he knew not what he said"; or of Caiaphas, who prophesied and proclaimed divine truths, without himself or his hearers understanding in the least what God's Spirit was saying through him? The remarkable story of Saul and of Balaam shows that the revelation of God appears even in the midst of idols and the very instruments of hell, and that he even uses them to be his servants and slaves, like Nebuchadnezzar.

An English divine was the first to try and introduce the unction of grace into natural philosophy. We still need a Derham to disclose to us not the God of naked reason, so to speak, but the God of Holy Scripture in the realm of nature; to show us that all nature's treasures are nothing but an allegory, a mythological picture of heavenly systems—just as all events of world history are silhouettes of more mysterious actions and disclosed miracles (Jer. 32. 20).

4

What question has given the sages of the world more trouble than that of the origin or admission of evil? God himself says, I create evil—if we had a right idea of things or tried to get one, then we should neither be led astray nor offended by mere expressions. Good and evil are really general concepts which do no more than indicate a relation of our self to other objects, and a reaction of this relation, so to speak, upon ourselves. We are therefore bound up with other things: on this nexus there rests not only our true being and real nature but also all the variations and nuances of which it is capable.

Our life needs to be maintained and restored by nourishment. This depends on the fruits of the earth, and they depend to some extent on the order of our industry and the course of nature. Laziness is therefore a moral evil, and increased prices a physical evil. But we call them both evils because they break the bond in which our existence and its preservation partly consist.

Our health is a good which consists in a harmony of the physical structure and its union with the soul. All that can destroy or change this is therefore called an evil; and on the other hand what can preserve or restore it is a good. Our health and life can cease to be a good when they invade a higher order which stands in a closer relation to our spiritual nature.

Man is a link in the chain of created things very remote from the great original being by whom all things exist and through whose Word they arose. No matter how weak a link he is in the whole nexus, yet everything depends upon God, and he who holds the chain in his hand bears man in his immediate care in virtue of the laws by which all mediated beings have their ground and their destiny in him.

Nothing sheds so extraordinary a light on the whole nature of things as the great truth of our Saviour, that none is good but God alone. Therefore instead of asking, whence comes evil? we should rather turn the question round and marvel that finite creatures are able to be good and happy. Here is the true mystery of the divine wisdom, love and omnipotence. This philosophical curiosity which wonders so much about the origin of evil, and is so disturbed by it, should be regarded almost as a dim awareness of the divine image in our reason, as a *hysteron proteron* the true meaning of which is seen when it is reversed, and in whose transposition there lies a cabbala, a secret understanding.

There is only a single bond which God makes into a law of our nature and its happiness. All that man does against this dissolves the general bond, the harmony, the peace which makes all external things too weak to affect him, and makes him strong enough to resist the violence of all objects which attack and oppress him; indeed, more than resist, himself to be master over their united power.

Imagine a powerful monarch who has sacrificed a favourite to the fury of his courtiers, that he may revenge himself on them by means of the son. The father is banished, and suddenly removed from the vengeance and power of his enemies. His son, not yet of age, remains in the kingdom, and everyone rages to torture the father doubly in the child, and to wreak a crueller vengeance in the heir. The monarch discloses the fate of the father to the child, the evil, the power and the cunning of his enemies, and a part of the secret why he cannot publicly declare himself for his father and him, why he must banish him from the court. At the same time he assures him that he may go everywhere without care; that he has arranged for an unknown friend to be with him everywhere and to watch his enemies' steps; that he will mark him with a sign which everyone must honour and which no one can erase or deprive him of—except his own hand or will, or disobedience and scorn of the warnings and helps the use of which he left to him; that his removal will last a short time; that he intends to lead him incognito to where his father is and, after certain important matters are settled, to call them both back publicly to his kingdom and declare them his friends and successors or co-rulers, and simultaneously punish their enemies.

Let us follow this child as his enemies lie in ambush for him. They do everything in their power to win him by caresses and by threats. They laugh at the sign on his brow, then they urge him to wash it off as a stain. They promise him tit-bits and mountains of gold if he will remove it of his own accord. Suppose that the enemies succeeded so far as to make it unrecognisable or temporarily invisible. They are merely waiting to give vent to their desire for revenge. Then, just when the child has discovered their cruelty and the danger he is in, the unknown friend comes to rescue him from their clutches. However short the way, he is threatened by inner anxiety and fear, and by the incessant attacks of his enemies; but his hitherto unknown friend always appears at the right moment to save him from destruction, and when he is present all nightmares and figures of danger vanish.

To take the parable a little further, let us suppose that the child bears a sign on his brow without knowing of it, and that only his own hand could remove it. It has therefore been impressed upon him that he must not touch his brow or be persuaded by any argument to do so, without his ever knowing the reasons, or the existence of the sign, or the respect his enemies have for it, but knowing only all the consequences of his disobedience.

The child is on his way—the monarch has given his promises and commands—he reaches the place where he is to find his father—he has the protection of the unknown friend on whom he is to rely in every danger: hope, child-like love and trust are his pride, his pleasure and his strength.

If we think of the human race and every man in a like case, that their life and security and eternal happiness depend upon a condition which triumphs over all difficulties, whereas its transgression not only forfeits their happiness but also brings them into the depths of misery, into constant fear, anxiety and danger, where they need salvation in each moment if they are not to be lost eternally—then we shall see the question about the origin of evil in a quite different light.

5

The more I reflect upon the idea of freedom, the more it seems to coincide with all my observations about it. I give two of them. It is agreed that there can be no freedom without laws; and we call those states free in which the people as well as the prince are subject to laws. Laws derive their whole force from the basic instinct of self-love, which makes rewards and punishments effective as causes. A law is never so disturbing and offensive as the sentence of a judge, however proper it is. A law does not touch my self-love at all, it is concerned with my action alone, and therefore treats me identically with everyone else in the same position. But an arbitrary sentence unrelated to law is always an imposition on us, which is resisted by the instincts of self-love. A law tells me the consequences of my action; hence the imagination cannot deceive us by any flattery or suspicions of the rightness of our prince or judge. Indeed in a free republic the judge shows me by his example that the law equally commands him to pronounce sentence on me and commands me to endure the sentence. Here then are the advantages of political freedom. Everyone knows the consequences of his actions, and no one can escape them, because only the will of the law can restrict me, and this will is as well known to me as it is unalterable. The will of the law is always before me, and supports my self-preservation and self-love. That is why we appeal to laws, and why we fear them. We may add that the laws which we impose on ourselves never seem hard to us, for the same reason of self-love; and it is the greatest prerogative of free states to be their own law-givers. Laws, therefore, do not limit freedom, but let me recognise the cases and the actions which will have advantageous or disadvantageous consequences for my self-love. This insight therefore determines our inclinations.

The Stoic principle that the virtuous man alone is free, and every evildoer is a slave, is also illuminated by this argument. Lust and vice hinder our knowledge; their false judgments confuse our self-love. We believe we are acting for the best, for our pleasure and honour, and we choose means which contradict these ends. Is this self-love? Where there is no self-love, there can be no freedom.

6

When one considers how much strength, presence of mind and rapidity, of which we are not normally capable, are given to us by the fear of an extraordinary danger, one understands why a Christian is so superior to the normal secure man, for he seeks his blessedness with constant fear and trembling.

7

My stomach complains at intemperance; every member has its feeling which warns it against what is harmful: this is a physical conscience.

8

What is the source of the respect in which the arts of divination are held, and of the great number of them which are based simply on a misunderstanding of our instinct or our natural reason? We are all capable of being prophets. All the phenomena of nature are dreams, visions, riddles, which have their significance, their secret meaning. The book of nature and the book of history are nothing but ciphers, hidden signs, which need the same key as unlocks Holy Scripture, and is the point of its inspiration.

9

The body is the garment of the soul. It covers its nakedness and shame. The voluptuous and the ambitious ascribe their vicious inclinations to their blood and fibres. The body serves to preserve the soul, just as clothing protects our body from the assaults of the air and other external powers. This need of our nature has preserved us, while higher, lighter spirits have fallen irredeemably. The hindrance of clothes, making us somewhat heavier and less able to use our limbs, is not so much a good thing in reference to the soul as in reference to evil. How abominable man might be, if the body did not keep him within limits!

10

The general good of a state is supported by the gifts of its subjects. Every fragment of industry is blessed by God for the general wealth and nourishment.

SOCRATIC MEMORABILIA

1759

This work, which Hamann himself said began his proper authorship, fills, in Nadler's edition, only twenty-five pages, of which five consist of the title-page and two dedications. However, titles and preliminary material were always as important as the rest of the book for Hamann—if not more important, sometimes. The work is an answer to Berens and Kant, who wanted to draw him away from the " regrettable religious exaggeration, superstition, enthusiasm, praying and folding of hands and confession," which they saw as the unfortunate outcome of his London experience. They wanted to make him useful, serviceable, part of the reasonable world. Hamann's answer is to oppose to the *Aufklärung* view of truth the view (which he supposes to be that of Socrates) that knowledge belongs not exclusively to the powers of the mind, but to the whole life committed to a continuity of thinking and action. However, Hamann makes Socrates in his own image, and in excusing himself from the " useful " literary work which Berens and Kant proposed to him, he praises Socrates for not having been an author—and in so doing he becomes an author after all, in his own way. The whole work is no more than an extended letter, an aphoristic, highly allusive and personal assertion of faith. Only a selection is given here, and the notes, moreover, have been treated with some freedom, where translation, reduction, or addition seemed to be a help to the English reader.

SOCRATIC MEMORABILIA

gathered together
for the whiling away of the public's time
by a lover of whiling away

With a double dedication
to nobody and two

O curas hominum! o quantum est in rebus inane!
Quis leget haec?   Min' tu istud ais?
            Nemo hercule—Nemo?
Vel DVO vel NEMO.

Persius

AMSTERDAM

1759

To the Public
or
Nobody, whom everybody knows

ὅδ' οὔτις, ποῦ 'στίν;[1]
Euripides, CYCLOPS

You bear a name, and do not need to prove your existence, you
meet with faith, and perform no signs to deserve it, you receive

[1] This nobody, where is he?

honour, and have no conception or feeling of it. We know that there are no idols in the world. Nor are you a man; yet you must be a human image which superstition has idolised. You lack neither eyes nor ears, but they do not see or hear, and the artificial eye you make, and the artificial ear you plant, are, like your own, blind and deaf.[1] You must know everything, and you learn nothing; you must judge everything, and you understand nothing; you are for ever learning, and you can never come to the knowledge of the truth.[2] You make poetry, have things to do, you are out and about, or perhaps asleep, when your priests call aloud, and you are meant to answer them and their scoffer with fire. Sacrifices are offered to you daily, which others consume at your expense, in order to give probability to your life by your mighty meals. Fastidious though you are, you are satisfied with everything, so long as no one appears before you with empty hands. Like the philosopher I throw myself at the benevolent feet of a tyrant. My gift is only some laxative pills, from which a god, like you, once burst.[3] So give them to a few of your worshippers, whom I wish by their means to purify from the service of your vanity.

Because you bear in your face the marks of human ignorance and curiosity I will confess to you who the two are on whom, through your hands, I will play this pious deceit. The first works at the stone of wisdom, like a philanthropist who regards it as a means of furthering the industry, the civic virtues and the welfare of public life. For him I have written in the mystical language of a sophist; for wisdom will always remain the most hidden mystery of politics, even though alchemy attains its goal of making all men rich, who must soon, with the aid of the Marquis of Mirabeau's fruitful maxims, populate all France. In the present plan of the world the art of making gold remains therefore

---

[1] Prov. 9. 13.   [2] II Tim. 3. 7.
[3] An allusion to Vespasian and his sigh of relief, *uti puto, deus fio.*

rightly the supreme project and supreme good of our clever statesmen.[1]

The other would like to figure as just as universal a sage and mint-master as Newton was.[2] No part of the critique is more certain than that which has been invented for gold and silver. Hence the confusion in the coinage of Germany cannot be as great as has crept into the school-books in current use. We lack proper conversion tables to decide of what weight and purity of metal an idea must be if it is to be reckoned a truth, and so on.[3]

Since these pills must be swallowed, not chewed, like those which the Medicis put in their coat-of-arms, they are not made for tasting. As for their effect, it was with a similar feeling that Vespasian first got to know the pleasure of your name, when he is said to have cried out, from a seat that was not his throne, *uti puto, deus fio.*

To the Two

σμικρὰ μὲν τάδ', ἀλλ' ὅμως ἄχω[4]

Sophocles in ELECTRA, 450

The public in Greece read Aristotle's thoughts on the natural history of animals, and Alexander understood them. Where a common reader might see nothing but mould, the emotion of friendship will perhaps disclose to you, gentlemen, a microscopic forest in these pages.

I have written about Socrates in Socratic fashion. Analogy[5] was the soul of his arguments, and he embodied them in irony.

---

[1] The first of the two to whom the work is dedicated is Hamann's patron and friend, J. C. Berens. H. breaks with him because he cannot accept the Enlightenment view of man which Berens typifies.

[2] The second of the two is Immanuel Kant. Kant's ambition appears to H. to be similar to that of Berens, only in the field of philosophy: Kant wants to assay ideas as though they were gold and silver coins.

[3] Cf. Euripides, *Medea*, 516ff.: " O Zeus, why hast thou granted to men means of assaying base currency, but to recognise a man as base, for that he is born with no mark on his body."

[4] A small thing, but mine own.

[5] " Analogy, man's surest guide below." Young, *Night Thoughts*, 6.

My uncertainty and confidence can be as peculiar as they want; here they must be regarded as æsthetic imitations.

In the works of Xenophon there is a superstitious piety, in Plato's an enthusiastic piety; therefore through all parts of this mimic work there runs a vein of similar sentiments. It would have been easiest for me to come closer to these pagans in their openness; but I have had to content myself with borrowing for my religion the veil which a patriotic St. John and a Platonic Shaftesbury have woven for their unbelief and misbelief.

Socrates, gentlemen, was no common critic. In the writings of Heraclitus he distinguished between what he understood and what he did not understand, and from what he understood he made a proper and modest supposition about what he did not. He spoke on this occasion of readers who could swim.[1] A flowing together of ideas and sentiments in that living elegy of the philosopher perhaps made the sentences into a mass of little islands, which were not joined by any bridges or ferries in their method.

Since you are both my friends, your partisan praise and your partisan blame will be alike acceptable to me. I am etc.

Introduction

The history of philosophy has had a fate similar to that of the statue of the French minister of state. A great artist[2] proved the skill of his chisel on it; a monarch,[3] who gave his name to a whole century, provided the costs for the monument and admired his subject's creation; but the Scythian[4] who was a travelling journeyman, and like Noah or the Galilean of the projector Julian became a carpenter in order to be the God of his people—this Scythian gave way to a weakness the memory of

---

[1] *Atque hic tam docilis ad cetera, natare nesciit.* Sueton. *de Caligula* (" And he, so apt in everything, could not swim.").

[2] Girardon.   [3] Louis XIV.   [4] Peter the Great.

which alone could perpetuate his name. He ran up to the marble statue, and magnanimously offered half of his large kingdom to the dumb stone[1] if it would teach him how to rule the other half. If our history were to become mythology this embrace of a lifeless teacher, who had performed miracles of fulfilment without personal profit, would be transformed into a fairy-tale that would be similar to the memories of Pygmalion's life. A creator of his people in the language of our understanding will after an unthinkable age have to be understood as poetically as a sculptor who models his wife . . .

As nature has been given to us to open our eyes, so history has been given to us to open our ears. To dismember a body and an event into its elements means to try to lay hold of God's invisible being, his eternal power and godhead. He who does not believe in Moses and the prophets will always be a poet, against his knowledge and desire, as Buffon in writing the story of creation and Montesquieu the story of the Roman empire . . .

I am surprised that so far no one has ventured to do as much for history as Bacon has done for physics. Bolingbroke advises his pupil to study ancient history as heathen mythology, like a poetic dictionary. Yet perhaps the whole of history is more mythology than this philosopher thinks, and like nature a sealed book, a cloaked witness, a riddle which cannot be solved unless we plough with some other ox than our reason . . .

Let us suppose that we suggest a game of cards to a man we do not know. If he were to say, " I don't play," we should either have to interpret it to mean that he does not understand the game, or that he objects to playing, for economic or moral or other reasons. But suppose an upright man of whom one knew that he was a very good player who knew both the rules and the illegal tricks very well, but loved the game and played it only as

[1] Habakkuk 2. 19.

an innocent pastime. He is challenged to a game by a set of clever cheats who are accounted good players, and to whom he is equal in both regards. If he says, " I don't play," we should have to look with his eyes at the people with whom he is speaking, and could complete what he says as follows: " I don't play, that is, with people of your kind, who break the rules and force the luck. When you offer me a game, then our mutual understanding is that we accept arbitrary chance as our master. But what you call chance is the science of your slick fingers, and I must accept this, if I will, or run the risk of insulting you, or choose the shame of imitating you. Had you offered a trial to see who the best cheat was then I might have replied differently, and perhaps joined you in a game in order to show you that you have learned to deal cards as badly as you know how to play what you do have." The views of Socrates may be put in these raw accents when he said to the sophists, the learned men of his time, " I know nothing." That is why these words were a thorn in their flesh and a scourge on their backs. All the ideas of Socrates, which were thrown out as a piece of his ignorance, seemed as terrible to them as the hair on Medusa's head, the centre of the ægis.

The ignorance of Socrates was sensibility. But between sensibility and a proposition is a greater difference than between a living animal and its anatomical skeleton. The old and new sceptics may wrap themselves as much as they please in the lion-skin of socratic ignorance, they still betray themselves by their voices and their ears. If they know nothing, does the world need a learned proof of it? Their hypocrisy is ridiculous and shameless. But he who needs so much quickness and eloquence to convince himself of his own ignorance must have in his heart an immense opposition to the truth of his ignorance.

Our own being and the existence of all things outside us must be believed[1] and cannot be established in any other way. What

---

[1] " The pupil must believe," Aristotle, *Soph. elencth.* I, 2.

is more certain than the end of man, and of what truth is there a more general and better confirmed knowledge? Yet no one is so clever as to believe this save he, as Moses gives us to understand, who is taught by God himself to consider that he must die. What one believes has for that reason no need to be proved, and a proposition can be irrefutably proved without for that reason being believed.

There are proofs[1] of truths which are of as little value as the application one can make of the truths;[2] in fact one can believe the proof of a proposition without approving the proposition. The reasons of a Hume may be ever so well grounded, and the refutation of them just borrowed propositions and doubts; so faith wins and loses just as much with the most adept babbler and the most honourable and objective pleader. Faith is not a work of reason and therefore cannot succumb to any attack by reason; because believing happens as little by means of reasons as tasting and seeing.

Relation and agreement of ideas is the same thing in a demonstrative proof as connection and symmetry of numbers and lines, sounds and colours in musical composition and painting. The philosopher is just as much subject to the law of imitation as the poet. For the poet his muse and its hieroglyphic shadow-play is as true as reason and its structures for the philosopher. If fate sets the greatest sage and the poet in circumstances where they really feel for themselves, the one denies his reason and discloses that he does not believe in the best of all possible worlds, however well he can prove it, while the other sees himself deprived of his muse and guardian angel when his Meta dies.[3] The imaginative power,

---

[1] " We propose two kinds of persuasion: one the persuasion of faith without knowing, the other the persuasion of knowledge." *Gorgias.*

[2] A philosopher gave such persuasive reasons for the immortality of the soul that his hearers joyfully committed suicide, as Lactantius tells us. Augustine, *de Civit. Dei* I, 22; Cicero, *Tusc. Quaest.* I, 39.

[3] Klopstock was inconsolable after the death of his young wife, Meta.

though it were a sun-horse and had the wings of the dawn,[1] therefore cannot be the creator of faith.[2]

For Socrates's witness to his ignorance I know no more honourable seal and no better key than the oracle of the great teacher of the heathen:

And if any man think that he knoweth anything, he knoweth nothing yet as he ought to know. But if any man love God, the same is known of him[3] —

as Socrates was known of Apollo to be a wise man. But as the corn of all our natural wisdom is bound to decay and pass away in ignorance, and as the life and being of a higher knowledge burst forth new-created from this death and nothingness—a sophist's nose does not reach as far as this. No mole-hill, but a tower of Lebanon is needed, which looks towards Damascus.[4]

What is the substitute in Homer for ignorance of the rules of art which Aristotle thought out later, and what is the substitute in Shakespeare for his ignorance or transgression of those critical rules? Genius is the unanimous answer. It was certainly all right for Socrates to be ignorant: he had a *genius* on whose knowledge he could rely, whom he loved and feared as his god, with whose peace he was more concerned than with all the reason of the Egyptians and Greeks, whose voice he believed and through whose breath (as the expert Dr. John Hill has proved[5]) the empty understanding of a Socrates can be made fruitful as well as the womb of a pure virgin.

. . . He who cannot live on crumbs and alms, or by robbery, and

---

[1] " Faith has this in common with twilight, that for both an admixture of darkness is necessary, when with increasing light faith passes into knowledge and twilight into daylight. Certain mysteries, in which faith carries the prize over the intellect, can more happily than the intellect prepare the way for the engendering of faith." Boyle, *Cogitationes*.

[2] Socrates in the *Phaedrus*.   [3] I Cor. 8. 2-3.   [4] Song of Sol. 7. 4.

[5] In *Lucina sine concubitu*, 1750 (a satire on the Royal Society and on Buffon's views of human procreation).

cannot give up everything for a sword,[1] is not fit for the service
of the truth; let him early become a reasonable, serviceable and
well-behaved man in the world, or learn how to bow and scrape
and lick plates—then he is safe for life from hunger and thirst,
from the gallows and the wheel.

If it is true that God himself, as it says in the good confession
he made before Pilate—if it is true, I say, that God himself became
a man and came into the world in order to bear witness to the
truth, it would need no omniscience to see beforehand that he
would not get out of the world as well as a Socrates, but would
die a more shameful and cruel death than the parricide of the
most Christian king, Louis the Well-beloved, who was a great-
grandson of Louis the Great.

[1] Cf. Aristophanes, *Clouds*, 1064ff.: " A sword! A fine prize—but Hyperbolos was so
bad that by means of his lamps he has got a great deal of money—but no, by Zeus,
no sword."

A CLOVER-LEAF
OF HELLENISTIC LETTERS

1759-60

The first Letter deals with the language and style of the New Testament. The main point is that a knowledge of classical Greek is not enough for the understanding of these writings. But a knowledge of what language and style really are, and a knowledge of the life which is represented in the New Testament, are the basic requirements. The second Letter is a plea for the study of Greek literature, not as the acquisition of learning, but to nourish life. Only some extracts from these first two Letters are given here.

A CLOVER-LEAF
OF HELLENISTIC LETTERS

First Letter

EVERY WAY of thinking which becomes a little fashionable, every imperceptible transition of the passions colours the expression of our ideas. The way of Christians (at all times reviled as a sect) must accordingly receive a new tongue and a holy style to distinguish it. Enter any community of Christians you like: the language in the holy place will betray its fatherland and genealogy, heathen branches grafted against nature on a Jewish stem . . . In brief, the oriental in our pulpit style leads us back to the cradle of our race and our religion, so that one must not resent the æsthetic taste of some Christian spokesmen . . .

It is part of the unity of the divine revelation that the Spirit of God lowered himself, and emptied himself of his majesty, in the human style of holy men who were impelled by him, just as the Son of God lowered himself in the form of a servant, and as the whole creation is a work of the utmost humility . . .

If therefore the divine style chooses the foolish, the shallow, the ignoble, to put to shame the strength and ingenuity of all profane writers, there certainly is need of the illuminated, enthused and eager eyes of a friend, an intimate, a lover, in order to discern through such a disguise the beams of heavenly glory. *Dei dialectus soloecismus*, says a well-known commentator. Here too it holds that *vox populi, vox Dei* . . .

The style of newspapers and letters, according to all rhetoricians, is the humble style of speaking, of which few analogies have survived in the Greek language. The style of the writings of the New Testament must, however, be judged according to this manner, and in this they are to some extent original.

Acts and Revelation are historical writings in the proper sense. Of the style in which future events must be presented we have nothing isoperimetrical except perhaps fragments of Delphic and Sibylline oracles.

Second Letter

... After the poets and the philosophers I come to the historians. One almost requires the same sagacity and *vis divinandi* for reading the past as for the future. As one begins the New Testament in school with the Gospel of John, so historians are regarded as the easiest writers. But can one know the past when one does not even understand the present? And who can have right ideas of the present without knowing the future? The future determines the present, and the present determines the past, as the purpose determines the constitution and the means to be used. Yet here we are accustomed to a *hysteron proteron* in our thinking, using our actions, like images in the eye, to turn around every moment without even noticing what we are doing ...

I should sooner regard anatomy as a key to knowing oneself than seek the art of living and governing in our historical skeletons, as they tried to tell me in my youth. The field of history has always seemed to me to be like that wide field that was full of bones, and behold, they were very dry. Only a prophet can prophesy of these bones that veins and flesh will grow on them and skin cover them. They have still no breath in them, till the prophet prophesies to the wind and the word of the Lord speaks to the wind ...

... Fury deprives me of all power of reflection when I think how such a noble gift of God as the sciences are laid waste, torn apart in coffee-houses by strong minds, trampled into academic messes by lazy monks, and how it is possible that young people can fall in love with that old crone, learning, who has no teeth or hair except possibly false ones. Διάπειρά τοι βροτῶν ἔλεγχος.[1]

[1] A trial for you, the scorn of men.

THE WISE MEN FROM THE EAST
IN BETHLEHEM
1761

The immediate occasion of this brief essay (here given in full) was the simultaneous preparation for two expeditions in 1761—one, the first voyage of Captain Cook to the southern seas to observe the transit of Venus through the solar orbit, and two, the mission planned by the redoubtable orientalist, Johann David Michaelis of Göttingen, to Arabia for the study of the customs and language. The search for the star, and the search for information from the east which might throw light on biblical antiquities, raised in Hamann's mind the image of the kings who followed a star in search of truth. The theme of Kierkegaard's *Fear and Trembling*—the exceptional and paradoxical life of faith, in which extraordinary and even reprehensible happenings, foolish in their motivation, disastrous in their outcome, are possible—is found here in miniature. A characteristic Hamannian turn of thought lies in the analogy between the life of faith and the life of the artist: genius, which is of divine origin, is the gift received by the exceptional man, whether he is a believer or an artist.

THE WISE MEN FROM THE EAST
IN BETHLEHEM

Τί ἂν θέλοι ὁ ΣΠΕΡΜΟΛΟΓΟΣ οὗτος λέγειν;
" What would this babbler say? "

Incipe parve pver risv cognoscere matrem

This year, at whose end we now stand, the reports of two learned societies have been given to the public, the first concerning an astronomical phenomenon which has already been reported and stimulatingly treated in our pages of queries and announcements;[1] the second concerns Oriental literature, which can enrich both the history of the human race and the antiquities of the Christian religion with many anecdotes.

My thoughts at present come to rest on the place where the little child was whose mysterious birth excited the curiosity of the angels and the shepherds, and to whose worship the Wise Men from the East, led by a strange guide, hastened to Bethlehem. Their joy at having at last reached the goal of their pilgrimage was doubtless expressed in solecisms such as are peculiar to violent and sudden passions.

If the muse of a successful poet who was also a clear-minded critic has dared to celebrate in a musical play the shepherds' visit

[1] The remarkable and long-awaited rare transit of Venus through the solar orbit, as this will occur on our Königsberg horizon on the morning of 6 June, 1761, with especial clarity and eagerly desired for astronomical observation, as calculated by an admirer of this fair science with the help of various astronomical tables, and printed as an invitation to his fellow-admirers for the observing of this important event by the baptised Jew, the surveyor.

to the manger, I may be permitted to kindle some grains of incense of Socratic thoughts to the memory of the Wise Men from the East.

Instead of basing an investigation on the doctrinal structure of some obscure sect and the ruins of its theogony and astrology; instead of a speculation about the magic star which would succeed neither algebraically nor in the manner of Fontenelle, I shall restrict myself to a general consideration of the morality of their journey.

Human life appears to consist of a series of symbolic actions by means of which our soul is able to reveal its invisible nature, and produces outside of itself, and communicates, a sensible knowledge of its real existence.

The mere body of an action can never disclose its value to us; but the representation of its causes and its consequences are the most natural mediating ideas by means of which our conclusions, along with the accompanying applause or displeasure, are produced.

This law of experience and reason does not seem to be favourable to the journey of our pilgrims, if the journey were to fall within the scope of their decision. What motivated their arrival, according to their own words, presses upon our judgment a long outmoded illusion, the impression of a legend to which they clung as a firm prophetic word—not to mention the abuse and the injustice which they perpetrated as citizens upon their fatherland by the extravagant worship of a foreign lord. As for the consequences of their undertaking, it may easily be supposed that the mothers who had to mourn the blood-bath of their children also lamented the heedless and meddlesome spirit of these strangers. The new-born king of the Jews himself had to take to flight, because he was betrayed by his worshippers to Herod, the reigning anti-Christ, a liar and murderer from the start.

Tremble, deceived mortals, who justify yourselves by the nobility of your intentions! The system of this year, which dispenses you from proving your premisses, will be the fairy-tale of next year. Take courage, deceived mortals, who despair at the evil consequences of your good works, and feel the stings of your victory! The will of providence must be more urgent for you than the arrogance of your contemporaries and of posterity.

Yet let us not esteem the truth of things according to the ease with which we can represent it to ourselves. There are actions of a higher order for which no equation in the elements (the ordinances) of this world can be produced. For it is the divine, which turns the wonders of nature and original works of art into signs, that distinguishes the morals and deeds of the holy who are called. Not only the end, but the whole pilgrimage of a Christian, is the workmanship[1] of the unknown genius whom heaven and earth recognise, and will recognise, as the one creator, mediator and preserver, in glorified human form.

Our life, we read, is " hidden with Christ in God. But when Christ—our life—will reveal himself, then we too shall be revealed with him in glory." And elsewhere we read, therefore the world does not know you, for the world does not know him. It is not yet manifest what we shall be. But we know that when it is manifest we shall be like him, for we shall see him as he is. Yes. He will come, that he may appear in glory with his holy ones, and wonderful with all believers.

How infinitely will the delight of those who love his coming exceed the exalted joy of our enthusiasts from the east when they saw the star! How emphatically, and how simply, does the original Scripture of our faith say

ἐχάρησαν χαρὰν μεγάλην σφόδρα.
" They rejoiced with exceeding joy."

[1] Eph. 2. 10.

לִישׁוּעָתְךָ קִוִּיתִי יְהוָֹה

"I have waited for thy salvation O Lord."

ἔτι γὰρ μικρον ὅσον ὅσον, ὁ ΕΡΧΟΜΕΝΟΣ ἥξει καὶ οὐ χρονίσει.

"For yet a little while, and the coming one shall come and shall not tarry."

Königsberg, 27/16 December, 1760

ÆSTHETICA IN NUCE

1762

This piece (of which only a few passages are translated here) appeared in 1762 as the chief item in the *Kreuzzüge des Philologen* ("Crusades of the Philologian"). It has as sub-title "A Rhapsody in Cabbalistic Prose." The rhapsodists, "the interpreters of the interpreters," according to Plato in the *Ion*, indicate the Greek aspect, the cabbala indicates the Hebrew aspect, the mysterious and symbolic: Hamann regards himself in this writing as the interpreter of the interpreters of God. It is therefore the æsthetic of the first author, the "poet at the beginning of days," God himself, which Hamann presents. Nature, history, and revelation are all alike words which God utters, and which point back to their divine author. In its immediate effect the *Æsthetica in Nuce* broke new ground for poetic activity in Germany, in the life of nature, the senses and passions. But its intention is wider, and includes an expansive view of revelation as being likewise unfettered by human rules, least of all by the rationalist and utilitarian norms of the eighteenth century.

ÆSTHETICA IN NUCE

NOT LYRE or paint-brush, but a corn-shovel for my muse, to sweep the barn of holy literature! Hail to the archangel over the relics of the language of Canaan! On fair asses[1] he is victorious in the race; but the wise fool of Greece borrows Euthyphron's proud stallions for the philological exchange of words.[2]

Poetry is the mother-tongue of the human race, as the garden is older than the field, painting than writing, song than declamation, parables than inferences,[3] barter than commerce. The rest of our earliest forebears was a deeper sleep; and their movement was a tumultuous dance. Seven days they sat in the silence of reflection or astonishment; and opened their mouths to utter winged words. Senses and passions speak and understand nothing but images. The whole treasure of human knowledge and happiness consists of nothing but images. The first outburst of creation, and the first impression of its historian, the first appearance and the first enjoyment of nature, are united in the words, Let there be light. Herewith begins the experience of the presence of things.[4]

Finally God crowned the revelation of his glory to the senses by the master-work of man. He created man in divine form— in the image of God he created him. This decree of the creator loosens the most complicated knots of human nature and its destiny. Blind heathens have recognised the invisible nature which men have in common with God. The veiled figure of the body,

[1] Judges 5. 10.   [2] See Plato's *Cratylus*.
[3] "As hieroglyphics are older than letters, so parables are older than arguments," says Bacon, my Euthyphron.
[4] "Anything that becomes visible is light," Eph. 5. 13.

196

the countenance of the head, and the extremities of the arms are the visible scheme in which we move; yet they are really nothing but a pointer to the hidden man within us.

Exemplumque Dei quisque est in imagine parva.[1]

The earliest nourishment came from the plant realm; the milk of the ancients was wine; the oldest poetic art was called botanic[2] by its learned scholiast (according to the fable of Jotham and Joash[3]); and man's first clothing was a rhapsody of fig-leaves ...

Speak that I may see thee! This wish was fulfilled in the creation, which is a speaking to the creature through the creature; for day unto day uttereth speech, and night unto night sheweth knowledge. Their line is gone out through all the earth to the end of the world, and there is no speech or language, where their voice is not heard. No matter where the fault is (outside us or within us), in nature we have nothing but a confusion of verses and *disiecti membra poetæ* left for our use. To collect them is for the scholar; to expound them, for the philosopher; to imitate them[4] or even more audaciously to bring them into order is the poet's modest part.

Speech is translation—from the language of angels into a language of men, that is, thoughts into words, things into names, images into signs, which can be poetical or kyriological,[5] historical or symbolical or hieroglyphical, philosophical or characteristic.[6]

---

[1] Manilius, *Astronomica* IV (" Each is an illustration of God in a small image.").

[2] " Since poetry is a plant, which has germinated as it were from the luxuriant earth and from a sure seed, it has increased beyond other learning and spread through them," Bacon, *de Augm. Scient.* II, 13.

[3] Judges 9. 7ff.; II Chron. 25. 18ff.

[4] Rescisso discas componere nomine versum;
Lucili vatis sic imitator eris. Ausonius, Epist. V.
(" Learn to compose a verse from a dismembered word;
Thus you will be an imitator of the poet Lucilus.")

[5] H. refers in a note to J. G. Wachter, *Naturæ & Scripturæ Concordia*, and Nadler in his Glossary quotes from V §1: " so far Scripture was a speaking drawing "—*scil.* of *the Lord.*

[6] Instead of H.'s note on Petronius and the Phaedrus I give Nadler's note from the Glossary: " H. speaks of the signs which reproduce pictures in a simplified form, and refers to the demotic cursive writing of the Egyptians. So he rightly says that these

This kind of translation (that is, speech) is, more than any other, like the underside of a carpet,

And shews the stuff, but not the workman's skill;

or like an eclipse of the sun, which can be seen in a bowl of water . . .

The book of creation contains examples of general ideas, which God desired to reveal to the creature by means of the creature; the books of the covenant contain examples of secret articles which God desired to reveal to man by means of man. The unity of the author is reflected in the very dialect of his works—in them all there is a single accent of immeasurable height and depth! A proof of the most glorious majesty and completest emptying! A miracle of such infinite calm making God to be like nothing, that one must in conscience deny his existence or be a beast;[1] but at the same time of such infinite power, filling all in all, that one does not know where to turn from the intensity of his activity towards us . . .

All the colours of the fairest world fade, as soon as you extinguish that light, the first-born of creation. If your stomach is your god, the very hairs of your head are in his guardianship. Every creature is in turn your sacrifice and your idol. Subject against its will—but still hoping—it sighs in its servitude or over your vanity. It does its best to escape your tyranny and, amid the most passionate embraces, longs for that freedom with which the beasts paid homage to Adam, when God brought them to the man to see what he would call them. For whatever he called them, that was their name.

---

cursive simplifications of pictures are like the underside of carpets, and have an unclear and confusing effect compared with the clear pictures of the top of the carpet. And this is what is meant when he says that the establishment of this content could have the effect of a satire on his own style, which reproduces pictures in demotic cursive writing."

[1] Psalm 73, 22.

This analogy of man to the Creator gives to all creatures their content and their character, from which depend loyalty and faith in the whole of nature. The livelier this idea, the image of the invisible God in our heart, the more capable we are of seeing and tasting, looking at and grasping with our hands, the loving-kindness of God in the creatures. Every impression of nature in man is not only a memento but also a pledge of the basic truth— who the Lord is. Every reaction of man towards the creature is a letter and a seal of our share in the divine nature, and that we are of his race.

O for a muse like a refiner's fire, and like fullers' soap![1] She will dare to purify the natural use of the senses from the un-natural use of abstractions, which mutilate our ideas of things as badly as they suppress and blaspheme the name of the Creator. I speak with you, O Greeks, because you think yourselves wiser than the chamberlains with the gnostic key;[2] just try to read the *Iliad* after excising, by abstraction, the vowels alpha and omega, and then tell me what you think of the poet's understanding and harmonies.

Apostille

As the oldest reader of this rhapsody in cabbalistic prose I consider myself bound by the right of the first-born to leave for my younger brothers, who will come after me, the following merciful judgment:

Everything in this æsthetic nut tastes of vanity—of vanity. The rhapsodist[3] has read, observed, reflected, he has sought and found pleasant words, faithfully quoted them, like a merchant ship he has fetched his provisions from afar. He has added

---

[1] *Malachi* 3. 2.
[2] Nadler (Glossary *ad. loc.*) writes: " H. means the ' chamberlains ' of Christ, who, like the evangelists and apostles, have the true key to the secret of the Lord."
[3] " The rhapsodists, the interpreters of the interpreters," Plato, *Ion.*

sentence to sentence, as one counts the arrows on a battle-field; and has measured off his figures of speech like the pegs of a tent . . .

Let us hear the sum of his latest æsthetic, which is also the oldest of all:

Fear God and give him the honour, for the time of his judgment is come, and pray to him who has made heaven and earth and sea and wells of water!

NEW APOLOGY OF THE LETTER H

BY ITSELF

1773

This piece, given here in full, appeared in 1773 as a kind of
envoi to a longer piece on the same theme. The defence of
the letter h in German orthography was undertaken by
Hamann in response to an attack upon it by a Wolffian
scholar. He makes it the occasion for a witty attack upon
the worship of reason and the attempt to ban the Spirit
from orthodoxy. Hamann wants to retain the significant
aspirate in spelling, as he clings to the Spirit in Christianity.

NEW APOLOGY OF THE LETTER H
BY ITSELF

YOU LITTLE prophets of Bohemian Breda![1] Do not be surprised that I speak to you with a human voice, like that dumb beast of burden, in order to punish your trespass. Your life is what I am—a breath. So do not think that I should crawl before you, whine to be retained, or lament at being banished or eradicated from your writings. I regard it as an honour and benefit to be less subject to the service of your vanity than my fellow vowels and consonants.

My existence and preservation are the affair of him who bears all things by the power of his Word, and has sworn and said, " Till heaven and earth pass, neither the smallest letter nor a tittle shall pass."

You little prophets of Bohemian Breda! I see that at all points you are all too superstitious. The invisible God (who is therefore unknown to you) is certainly the Father of reason and religion, which are, however, spirit and truth, and therefore as hidden from your senses as the invisible God (who is therefore unknown to you).

" What eye has not seen, nor ear heard, nor has entered into the heart of man "—this is what the only religion consists of which is worthy of a supreme being and becoming to him, and which God has prepared for them that love him.

But is human love possible without knowledge and sympathy?

---

[1] *Le petit prophète de Boehmischbroda* is the title of a book by F. M. Grimm which attacks French music and opera.

You boast that you know God. How did you reach this laudable knowledge? Through consideration of his works? How do you know that these works know him better than you do, and are they not much less capable than yourselves of this high revelation, and of communicating it to you? In order yourself to get to know a mere man—and the most familiar of all—would you depend on outer works? How dissimilar, how remote and strange, indeed how contradictory are these works to the depths of the inward man which are hidden in the heart!

So do not lie against the truth with your vainglorious knowledge of God. For lies are part of the wisdom which is earthly, human and devilish. For all the propositions of your so-called general, healthy and expert reason are lies—more incomprehensible, contradictory and barren than all the mysteries, miracles and signs of the most holy faith, which you persecute as vainly as this most extraordinary religious teacher of your century, with his " casual thoughts in connection with the main theme," persecutes me, who speak to you, like that dumb beast of burden who sought to avert the folly of the prophet it carried, and who smote it in the ardour of his unbelief or of his even more exaggerated credulity.

You little prophets of Bohemian Breda! In order really to produce the knowledge of the supreme being upon your little wandering star, as you yourself call it, I suppose there is no more natural and reasonable means left but for one of your brothers to go up to heaven, and descend again into the abyss of the dead; for God is not a God of the dead, but of the living. But you are dead in life, and your true destiny is to pass through death to life.

Do not blaspheme with false tongue, which is kindled by hell and blackens the whole artificial mechanism of your mode of life. Your hatred of God, like his wrath towards you, is infinite; the worm of hatred does not die, the fire of wrath is not quenched.

Only speak of natural love of God when every body on your earth denies the force of inertia and the axioms of gravity at the sound of your miraculous voice.

All your inclinations, the imaginations of your heart from your youth up, tend towards the centre of the earth. Unhindered expression of your activity would remove you from the Father of lights into infinite emptiness, but for his higher, gracious, direct attractions from above; since all that is in the world is not of the Father but of the world. But you belong to the world, and you do not know the language and cannot hear the words of him who is not of the world.

You little prophets of Bohemian Breda! The object of your reflections and devotion is not God, but a mere word-image, like your universal human reason, which by a more than poetic licence you deify as a real person, making so many similar gods and persons by the transsubstantiation of your word-images that the crassest heathendom and blindest popery in comparison with your philosophical idolatry will be justified and perhaps acquitted on the day of judgment.

Is the nature of those word-images just as unknown to you as the jealous God, whose name and honour you violate like thieves and murderers—is your whole human reason anything else but tradition, and does it take much to trace the genealogy of your trivial, barren and twice-dead opinions back to the source? Is not your human reason an indeterminate organ, a waxen nose, a weather-cock, to which must be preferred the letter of a holy canon which was once written and has stood fast till now? Is the famous principle of the *coincidentia oppositorum* entirely unknown to you? It is the Spirit which makes alive; the letter is flesh, and your dictionaries are straw!

You little prophets of Bohemian Breda! What need to ask of you a solemn vow that you do not care a fig for posterity and truth, and that your chief good is the majority opinion and a superfluity of cash? You say, " our fathers taught the humdrum gait of their time, the ears of our generation are itching and we must scratch them." You hypocrites! Do you yourselves not bear witness that you are children of your fathers, and condemn both them and yourselves?

A pattern of his age, like Saul, and a groundling similar to him, may be fobbed off with the puppet-theatre of a dead prophet and an old crone; but to breathe such an apology as mine into such a little letter as I am is truly not your affair, you great prophets of Bohemian Breda!

A REVIEW OF KANT'S
CRITIQUE OF PURE REASON
1781
AND
METACRITIQUE
OF THE PURISM OF REASON
1784

The *Metacritique* (posthumously published in 1800) and the review of Kant's *Critique of Pure Reason* (1781) which here precedes it (both given in full) are intended as an attack upon Kant's epistemology. Both the review and the more elaborate (but still not detailed) *Metacritique* were withheld by Hamann from publication, out of deference to Kant, whom he never ceased to describe as his friend and benefactor. Hamann might have known better, for Kant was not in the habit of reading criticisms of his own work, and in fact once had three criticisms sent to Hamann, " for the inquisitive old man " to read. In Kant's work Hamann sees the development of a philosophy of reason from the πρῶτον ψεῦδος of divorcing knowledge from both experience and tradition. The *metacritique* which he ironically proposes is that language itself should now be purified. In speech and language Hamann finds the indispensable and inescapable source, structure and substance of all thinking, and by an examination of its nature he hopes to restore the broken link with experience and tradition. Or rather, more modestly, he hopes to show the way for "more capable brains" than his own to do this. A "grammar of reason," *i.e.*, of philosophy, he held to be possible only on the basis of a grammar of language, in the strongly empirical sense which he had learned from the British philosophers. However much he may have overstressed the apriorism of Kant's thought, and underestimated the significance of the transcendental æsthetic, it is possible to say that in these two works in particular, and in many scattered references throughout his letters and writings, Hamann is clearing the ground for a task which has only been taken up, and so far rather one-sidedly, by the linguistic philosophers of our own day.

A REVIEW OF KANT'S
CRITIQUE OF PURE REASON

" Our age is the real age of criticism, to which everything must
submit. Religion on account of its holiness, and law-giving on
account of its majesty, try to escape this criticism. But they
immediately awaken just suspicion, and cannot claim the unfeigned respect which reason accords only to that which is able
to withstand its free and public examination."

With unfeigned respect the present reviewer announces this
work, in order at least to further, by his limited notice, a free and
public examination among readers who are equal to the task, and
are fitted for it by leisure as well as taste.

Leibniz intellectualised the appearances, Locke turned the
concepts of the understanding into matters of sense, and pure
reason assimilates appearances and concepts, the elements of all
our knowledge, " to a transcendental something $=$ X, of which
we neither know nor can know anything at all, as soon as it is
separated from sense-data." Knowledge which is concerned not
with objects themselves, but with *a priori* concepts of objects, is
called transcendental, and the critique of pure reason is the
complete idea of a transcendental philosophy. Under this new
name superannuated metaphysics is suddenly transformed from a
two-thousand-year-old arena of endless strife into a systematically
arranged inventory of all that we possess by means of pure reason
—and rises on the wings of a rather abstract genealogy and
heraldry to the sovereign dignity and Olympian hope " of
experiencing, alone among the sciences, its absolute completion,

and moreover in a short space of time, without any magical arts" or magic talismen, as the wise Helvetius says, " but everything derived from principles," holier than those of religion, more majestic than those of law-giving. Nevertheless, the decision about the mere possibility or impossibility of a metaphysic depends still upon the many-sided and unexhausted question: what and how much can understanding and reason, free of all experience, know? What, and how much, may I hope to accomplish by means of the reason, when I am deprived of every material and contribution of experience? Is there human knowledge independent of all experience, are there forms independent of all material? What is the formal distinction between concepts *a priori* and concepts *a posteriori*? Is there really a secret hidden in the *differentia specifica* between analytic and synthetic judgments which did not occur to any of the ancients? Are *prius* and *posterius*, analysis and synthesis not natural correlates, and accidental opposites, but both of them grounded, like the receptivity of the subject to the predicate, in the spontaneity of our concepts? Are not *ideæ matrices* and *ideæ innatæ* children of one spirit? Do not sensibility and understanding, the two branches of human knowledge, spring from one common root, though unknown to us, the sensibility giving the objects, and the understanding thinking (understanding, conceiving) them? Why such a violent and unauthorised divorce of that which nature has joined together? Will not this dichotomy or cleavage of their transcendental root cause both branches to dry up and wither away?

Experience and matter are therefore the common or ordinary, which by being separated off allows the desired purity to be found, and the form which remains, as the possession of the reasoning faculty, is as it were the virgin soil for the future system of pure (speculative) reason under the title of Metaphysic of Nature, of which the present *Critique* is but the propædeutic. But since the whole content is bound to be only form without content, was any form better than the clumsy construction of the scholastic art-form, or any schematism purer than the synthesis of the syllogistic apodeictic tripod?

The two main divisions, a transcendental doctrine of elements and a transcendental doctrine of method, correspond to the determinable and its determination. Space and time, as the pure forms of sensibility *ab extra sicut ab intra*, with their empirical reality and transcendental ideality, are presented and explained, in the transcendental æsthetic, the first part of the doctrine of elements, as certainly and indisputably " as can ever be demanded of a theory which is to serve as an instrument." Transcendental logic falls, like general logic, into analytic and dialectic, though with the difference that transcendental logic, with its categories and amphibolies of a more modern system, is recommended as a more modest synonym for general ontology. But because formal purity, without content or object, must necessarily and " without any guilt " of its own, degenerate into illusory holiness, trans-cendental dialectic has the task of explaining this hereditary defect—as unrecognised as it is incurable—as the true *pudenda* of pure reason, namely its paralogisms in regard to the psycho-logical ego and its antinomy in regard to all cosmological ideas; carrying out this task by thesis and antithesis, like the marvellous war in the old hymn, in which " one death swallowed up the other." After this autocheiria or euthanasia pure reason finally penetrates to the ideal of its mystical unity as the regulative principle of its whole constitutive schematism and ethereal structure. The conclusion of the doctrine of elements forms a critique, worked out excellently and *con amore*, of all speculative theology, though the shrewd observation about Plato should be applied also to the law-giver and critic of pure reason himself.

The transcendental doctrine of method determines the formal conditions of a complete system of pure reason. It treats of the discipline of reason, which runs neatly parallel to the Pauline theory of the discipline of the law, in its canon, its architectonic, and its history, in the threefold consideration (1) of its object, where Christ appears as the head of the philosophy of sense, Plato as the head of the philosophy of intellect; (2) of the origin of pure knowledge of reason, where Aristotle is the head of the empiricists and again Plato leads the neologists; (3) of method. The naturalistic method is mere misology reduced to propositions, and falls into the absurdity of boasting its neglect of all artificial means as a method of its own. The scientific method is bound to proceed systematically. Christian Wolf among the dogmaticians, and David Hume among the sceptics, are *velut inter ignes Luna minores*. Only the critical way remained open—this new pathway seems as uncomfortable to be a road for armies, as a tight-rope is to be a common path. Indifferentism, " as an effect not of heedlessness but of a ripe power of judgment in our age," likes to pose as " critical ": but because " an artificial indifference to materials and objects which cannot be indifferent to human nature and its interest " is either a wanton deception of the worst hypocrisy, or is part of the phenomena of the fatal lethargy of the age, this indifferentism could properly be called hypocritical or even political, in opposition both to the sceptical anarchy, which in despair at the chaos of its method must give itself up to laziness, and to the dogmatic despotism, which goes to work by means of *hystera protera* or (if I may use a cynical South German expression) backside foremost, and uses the weapons of light to spread the kingdom of darkness and barbarism. To follow the same Abbé Terrasson who tried to appraise the æsthetic lie of transcendental writings not *ab extra* but *ab intra*, an author's happiness consists in " being praised by some and known by all," and the present reviewer adds as the maximum of genuine authorship and criticism, " to be understood by precious few."

O quantum est in rebus inane
sunt lacrumæ rerum.

1 *July*, 1781

METACRITIQUE
OF THE PURISM OF REASON

Sunt lacrumæ rerum
—O quantum est in rebus inane.

A GREAT philosopher has asserted that " general and abstract ideas are nothing but particular ideas, but bound to a certain word, which gives a greater scope or extension to their meaning, and at the same time reminds us of that meaning in individual things." This assertion of the Eleatic, mystic, enthusiastic Bishop of Cloyne, George Berkeley, is described by Hume as one of the greatest and most valuable discoveries made in our time in the republic of letters.

First and foremost, it seems to me that the new scepticism owes more to the older idealism than this casual, single occasion would incidentally give us to understand, and that without Berkeley Hume would scarcely have become the great philosopher which criticism, in unanimous gratitude, makes him out to be. And as for the important discovery itself, that lies open and exposed without any particular profundity, in the mere linguistic usage of the meanest perception and observation of the *sensus communis*.

The possibility of human cognition of objects of experience

213

without, and preceding, all experience, and consequent upon this, the possibility of sense-intuition preceding all experience of an object, belongs to the hidden mysteries the exploration of which, let alone the resolution of which, it has not entered any philosopher's heart to undertake. On this twofold *im*possibility, and the immense distinction between analytic and synthetic judgments, is based the material and form of a transcendental doctrine of elements and method. For besides the peculiar distinction of reason as an object or source of knowledge and reason as a mode of cognition, there is a still more general, sharp and pure distinction, in virtue of which reason underlies all objects, sources and modes of cognition, and is not itself any one of these three; consequently it has need neither of an empirical or æsthetic, nor a logical or discursive concept, but consists merely in subjective conditions in which everything, something and nothing can be thought as the object, source or mode of cognition, and can be given, if need be can be taken, as an infinite maximum or minimum for direct intuition.

The first purification of philosophy consisted in the partly misunderstood and partly unsuccessful attempt to render the reason independent of all tradition and belief in tradition. The second purification is even more transcendental, and results in nothing less than independence of experience and its everyday induction. —For after reason sought for over two thousand years one knows not what beyond experience, it not only despairs all at once of the progressive course of its forebears, but also defiantly promises impatient contemporaries, and moreover in a short time, that general and infallible philosopher's stone, essential for Catholicism and despotism, to which religion will straightway subject its holiness and the law its majesty—especially in the last decline of a critical century, in which ambiguous empiricism, stricken with blindness, makes its own nakedness more suspicious and ludicrous from day to day.

The third, chief, and as it were empirical purism concerns language, the only, the first and the last instrument and criterion of reason, with no other credentials but tradition and usage. But one has almost the same experience with this idol as the ancient philosopher had with the ideal of reason. The more one considers, the deeper and more inward is one's dumbness and loss of all desire to speak. " Woe to the tyrants, when God troubles himself about them! Why then do they question after him? Mene, mene, tekel, to the sophists! They are weighed in the balances, and are found wanting, and their exchanges are broken! "

Receptivity of language and spontaneity of ideas! From this twofold source of ambiguity pure reason draws all the elements of its disputation, its scepticism and its criticism; by an analysis as arbitrary as the synthesis of the thrice-aged leaven it breeds new phenomena and meteors of the changeable horizon, creates signs and wonders by means of the maker of all, the destructive Mercurial wand of its mouth, or with the split goose-quill between the three syllogistic writing-fingers of its Herculean fist.

This hereditary defect and leprosy of ambiguity clings to the very name of metaphysics, and is not removed, far less transfigured, through being traced to its birthplace in the casual synthesis of a Greek prefix. But even though it is granted that in the transcendental topic the empirical distinction of *behind* and *beyond* mattered still less than the *hysteron proteron* in an *a priori a posteriori*, yet the birth-mark of the name widens out from the brow to the very heart of all knowledge, and its terminology is related to that of every other speech—in art and in the fields, in the mountains and the schools—as quicksilver is related to the other metals.

From so many analytical judgments one should certainly infer a gnostic hatred of matter or a mystic love of form. Yet the synthesis of the predicate with the subject—in which the true object of pure reason consists—has as its central concept nothing more than an old and cold prejudice for mathematics before and behind it, whose apodeictic certainty rests chiefly on a, so to speak, literal description of the simplest and most sensible intuition, and on the ease with which it can confirm and represent its synthesis, and the possibility of it, in visible constructions or symbolic formulæ and likenesses whose sensible nature excludes all misunderstanding. But while geometry determines and fixes even the ideality of its concepts of points without parts, of lines and surfaces in dimensions which are also divided ideally, by means of empirical signs and images, metaphysics misuses all word-signs and figures of speech drawn from our empirical knowledge, and turns them into sheer hieroglyphs and types of ideal relations; by this learned mischief it works up straightforward language into such a senseless, ruttish, unstable, indefinite something $=$ X, that nothing is left but a rushing wind, a magic shadow-play, at most, as the wise Helvetius says, the talisman and rosary of a transcendental superstitious belief in *entia rationis*, their empty skins and rubble heaps. Lastly, it is to be understood that if mathematics can claim for itself the precedence of nobility on account of its general and necessary reliability, human reason must rank below the infallible and unerring instinct of the insects.

Therefore, if it is still a chief question, how the ability to think is possible—the ability to think right and left, before and without, with and beyond experience—then it needs no deduction to prove the genealogical priority of language and its heraldry over the seven holy functions of logical propositions and inferences. Not only does the whole ability to think rest upon language—to follow the ignored predictions and reviled achievements of the worthy Samuel Heincke—but language is also the central point of reason's misunderstanding of itself, partly on account of the coincidence of the greatest and smallest concept, its emptiness and fullness, in idealist propositions, partly on account of the endless figures of speech before the conclusions, and much more of the same sort.

Sounds and letters are therefore pure forms *a priori*, in which there is found nothing that belongs to the sensation or conception of an object, nothing of the true æsthetic elements of all human knowledge and reason. Music was the oldest language, and next to the palpable rhythm of the pulse and the breath in the nostril was the original bodily image of all measurement of time and its numerical relations. The oldest writing was painting and drawing, and was therefore concerned, just as early, with the economy of space, its limitation and determination by means of shapes. Hence the concepts of time and space, through the immense and continuous influence of the two noblest senses, sight and hearing, have made themselves as general and indispensable in the whole sphere of the understanding as light and air are for eye, ear and voice, so that space and time, though not *ideæ innatæ*, seem to be at least the *matrices* of all knowledge reached by intuition.

But if sensibility and understanding spring as two branches of human knowledge from one common root, so that through sensibility objects are given, through understanding they are thought, what is the use of such an arbitrary, improper and self-willed divorce of that which nature has joined together? Will not such a dichotomy or cleavage of their common root cause both branches to die and wither away? For an image of our knowledge would not a single tree-trunk be more appropriate, with two roots, one above in the air, and the other below in the earth? The former is exposed to our sensibility, the latter, on the other hand, is invisible, and must be thought by means of the understanding, which agrees more with the priority of what is thought and the posteriority of what is given or taken, as well as with the beloved inversion of pure reason in its theories.

There is still perhaps a chemist's tree of Diana, not only for the knowledge of sensibility and the understanding, but also for the explaining and extending of both realms and their limits, which by means of a pure reason, baptised *per antiphrasin*, and its metaphysics (that ancient mother of chaos and night in all the sciences of morality, religion and law), slavishly serving the dominant indifferentism, have been so obscured, confused and desolated, that only the dawn of the promised near re-creation and illumination can bring to re-birth the dew of a pure natural language.

Without waiting, however, for the visit of a new Lucifer from the heights, or seizing the fig-tree of the great goddess Diana, the wicked snake in the bosom of ordinary popular language gives us the finest parable of the hypostatic union of the two natures of sense and of understanding, the mutual commerce in idioms of their powers, the synthesised mysteries of the two corresponding and contradicting forms of *a priori* and *a posteriori*, together with the transubstantiation of subjective conditions and subsumptions into objective predicates and attributes by the *copula* of a word of power or an expletive to cut short boredom and to fill out the empty space in periodic galimatias by thesis and antithesis.

O for the action of a Demosthenes and his triune energy of eloquence or the mimic " still to come," without the pane-gyrically tinkling cymbal of an angel's tongue! Then I should open the reader's eyes, that he might perhaps see—hosts of intuitions rising up into the fortress of pure understanding and hosts of concepts descending into the deep abyss of the most palpable sensibility, on a ladder dreamt by no sleeper, and the figurative dance of this Mahanaim or two hosts of reason, the secret and offensive chronicle of their love-making and ravishing, and the whole theogony of gigantic and heroic forms of the Shulammite and muse, in the mythology of light and darkness, even including the metamorphoses of an ancient Baubo—

inaudita specie solaminis, as St. Arnobius says—and a new immaculate virgin, but who cannot be the Mother of God, as St. Anselm considered her to be——

Words, then, have an æsthetic and a logical capacity. As visible and audible objects they belong, with their elements, to sensibility and intuition, but in accordance with the spirit of their appointment and meaning they belong to the understanding and to concepts. Consequently words are both pure and empirical intuitions and pure and empirical concepts: empirical, because the sensation of sight or hearing is effective through them; pure, in so far as their meaning is not determined by anything belonging to those sensations. Words as indeterminate objects of empirical intuitions are called, in the basic text of pure reason, æsthetic appearances. Consequently, in accordance with the old tune of antithetic parallelism, words as indeterminate objects of empirical concepts are critical appearances, ghosts, non-words or un-words, and only become, by their appointment and their meaning in use, determinate objects for the understanding. This meaning and its determination arise, as is well known, from the joining of a word-sign which is *a priori* arbitrary and indifferent, but *a posteriori* necessary and indispensable, with the intuition of the object itself, and it is by means of this repeated bond of the word-sign and the intuition itself, that the concept is communicated to, impressed upon, and incorporated in the understanding.

Now on the one hand idealism asks whether it is possible to find the concept of a word from the mere intuition of it. Is it possible to produce something of the concept of the word *reason* (*Vernunft*) from the matter of the word, from its six letters or two syllables, or from the form of the word which determines these letters and syllables? Here the Critique gives the same reply with its two scales. Certainly in some languages there are words, more or less in number, out of which logogriphs, French charades and witty rebuses can be created by analysis and the use of the syllables in new forms. But these are then new intuitions and appearances of words which no more agree with the concept of the given word than do the different intuitions themselves.

On the other hand idealism asks, further, whether it is possible to find the empirical intuition of word from the understanding. Is it possible to find in the concept of reason the matter of its name, i.e. in German the eight letters or two syllables of *Vernunft*, or similarly in any other language? Here one scale of the Critique answers with a decided negative. But is it not possible to derive from the concept the form of its empirical intuition in the word, the form in virtue of which one of the two syllables stands *a priori*, and the other *a posteriori*; or is it not possible that the eight letters arranged in a definite relationship, may be intuited? Here the Homer of pure reason snorts as loud a yes as Hans and Grethe at the altar, presumably because he has dreamt that the universal character of a philosophical language, so long sought for, has at last been found.

This last possibility of drawing the form of an empirical intuition without object or sign out of the pure and empty quality of our outer and inner spirit, is the Δός μοι ποῦ στῶ and the πρῶτον ψεῦδος; it is the cornerstone of critical idealism and its tower and lodge of pure reason. The given or taken materials belong to the categorical and idealist woods, the peripatetic and academic larders. Analysis is nothing more than a cutting-up in line with the fashion, just as synthesis is no more than an artificial seam made by a master-tailor. For the sake of weak readers I have explained the metagrobolising[1] of transcendental philosophy with reference to the sacrament of language, the letter of its elements and the spirit of its appointment, and I leave it to each reader to unclasp the clenched fist and make it an open hand.

[1] A coinage of Rabelais (*mataia* = vain; *graphein* = to write; *bolizein* = to plumb). Hamann alters the first syllables to *meta*. The meaning is something like " nonsensical investigations."

Perhaps a similar idealism is the wall of partition between Judaism and heathendom. The Jew had the word and the signs, the heathen had reason and its wisdom (the consequence was a *metabasis eis allo genos*, of which the finest has been transplanted in the little *Golgotha*).

GOLGOTHA AND SCHEBLIMiNI

1784

A complete understanding of this work rests upon an understanding of Moses Mendelssohn's *Jerusalem*. Thus the title itself, with a general reference to the crucified and exalted Lord (cf. Psalm 110. 1: "sit thou at my right hand—Hebrew *scheblimini*) has also a particular reference to the real Jerusalem, which in Mendelssohn's book is just a ruined city. Hamann's violent reaction against Mendelssohn springs from his hatred of the religion of reason which Mendelssohn presents as the fitting partner of an enlightened state. In agreement with his friend Lessing, Mendelssohn regarded truths of reason, eternal propositions, as the fit material for a church whose role was to *teach* the people. The particular turn to Mendelssohn's argument lies in his transformation of Judaism into just such a teaching of general truths. Hamann takes up the argument of *Jerusalem* and by a remarkable combination of analysis and quotation, which can only be fully disentangled by exact study of Mendelssohn's text, he tries to bring out what seem to him to be the characteristic differences between Mendelssohn's (and the Enlightenment's) view and the historical Christianity which he himself stands for. In his emphases Hamann is very modern. The small selection which can be given here, without too pressing a need for commentary, reproduces Hamann's main theological assertions.

GOLGOTHA AND SCHEBLIMINI

by

A Preacher in the Wilderness

Moses

Who said of his father and mother,
    I regard them not;
He disowned his brothers,
    and ignored his children. . . .
They shall teach Jacob thy ordinances,
    and Israel thy law;
They shall put incense before thee,
    and whole burnt offerings upon thy altar.

Jeremiah

Behold, I will feed them with wormwood, and give them
poisoned water to drink; for from the prophets of
Jerusalem ungodliness has gone forth into all the land.

For he spoke, and it came to be—" and whatever the man called
every living creature, that was its name"; in accordance with this
model and image of definition every word of a man should be
and remain the thing itself. It is on this similarity of the impression
and the inscription to the pattern of our race and the master of
our youth, on this natural right to make use of the word, as the
most real, noble and powerful means of revelation and communication of our inmost declaration of the will, that the
validity of all contracts is founded, and the safe stronghold of the
hidden truth is superior to all French practice, tax-machinery,

224

pedantry and quackery. The misuse of language and its natural testimony is thus the crassest perjury, and turns the trespasser of this first law of reason and its justice into an arrant enemy of mankind, a traitor and opponent of German[1] uprightness and honourableness, on which our dignity and happiness rest . . .

Actions and dispositions are part of the true fulfilment of our duties and of the perfection of man. State and church have them both as their object. Consequently actions without dispositions and dispositions without actions are a halving of complete and living duties into two dead halves. If motives may no longer be grounds of truth, and grounds of truth no longer serve as motives, if the being depends on necessary understanding, and reality on accidental will, then all divine and human unity in dispositions and actions ceases. The state becomes a body without spirit and life—a carcase for eagles! The church becomes a ghost, without flesh and bone—a scarecrow for sparrows! Reason with its unchanging pattern of concepts, presupposing or excluding one another, stands still, like the sun upon Gibeon and the moon in the valley of Ajalon . . .

Because I too know of no eternal truths save those which are unceasingly temporal, I do not need to mount into the cabinet of the divine understanding nor into the sanctuary of the divine will; nor do I need to linger over the difference between direct revelation by means of Word and Scripture, which is only comprehensible here and now, and indirect revelation by means of the thing (nature) and the concept, which on account of their writing in the soul are supposed to be legible and comprehensible at all times and in all places.

---

[1] H. uses " German " as a synonym for " good " or " proper." He was one of the first exponents of the rising German national feeling, expressed mainly as anti-French, *i.e.*, against the French bureaucracy of Frederick the Great under which he personally suffered, and against the French rationalists.

" Always to resist all theories and hypotheses and speak of facts, to want to hear nothing but facts, and to watch out for facts least of all where it most matters "—but I am neither hungry for the shew-bread, nor have I leisure or strength for labyrinthine walks and peripatetic labyrinths. But I hasten to the point, and perfectly agree with Herr Mendelssohn that Judaism knows of no revealed religion, taking this in his own sense to mean that nothing has been confided by God to the Jews through Word and Scripture but the sense vehicle of the mystery, the shadow of good things to come and not the very being of the things, whose real communication was reserved for a higher Mediator, High-priest, Prophet and King than Moses, Aaron, David and Solomon. Thus just as Moses himself did not know that his face shone, making the people afraid, so the whole law-giving of this divine minister was a mere veil and curtain of the old religion of the covenant, which to this day is unlifted, wrapped up and sealed. The characteristic difference between Judaism and Christianity is neither direct nor indirect revelation, in the sense adopted by Jews and naturalists, nor is it eternal truths and dogmas, nor ceremonial laws and moral laws: the characteristic difference lies solely in temporal truths of history, which took place at one time and never recur—*facts* which have become true in a connection of causes and effects in one time and place, and thus can be thought of as true only from that time and place, and must be confirmed by authority. Authority, while it can humble, cannot teach. It can overthrow reason, but it cannot fetter it. Nevertheless, without authority the truth of history disappears along with the happening itself.

This characteristic difference between Judaism and Christianity concerns historical truths not only of past but also of future times, which are proclaimed in advance and prophesied by the Spirit of a universal and particular providence, and which by their nature can only be accepted by means of faith. Jewish authority alone provides them with the required authenticity; and these memorabilia of the past and the future world were confirmed by miracles and by the credibility of the witnesses and those who handed on the tradition; and they were supported by the evidence of real fulfilment which is sufficient to establish faith beyond the reach of all Talmudic and dialectical doubts and qualms.

Hence the revealed religion of Christianity is rightly called faith, trust, confidence, and hopeful and childlike assurance of divine pledges and promises and of the glorious progress of its developing life in representations from glory to glory, till the full revelation and apocalypse of the mystery which was kept secret and believed since the world began, in the fullness of seeing face to face: just as the father Abraham believed in the Eternal, and rejoiced to see his day, and he saw it and was glad; for he staggered not at the promise of God through unbelief, but was strong in faith, giving glory to God. Therefore it was counted to him for righteousness. But the law-giver Moses was denied entrance into the promised land; and by a similar sinfulness of unbelief in the spirit of grace and truth, which should have been preserved in hieroglyphic customs, symbolic ceremonies and actions of unalloyed meaning, until the time of refreshing, pouring out of the Spirit, and anointing, this earthly vehicle of a temporal, imaged, dramatic, animal law-giving and sacrificial worship degenerated into the corrupted and deadly creeping poison of a childish, slavish, literal, idolatrous superstition. Accordingly Moses with all the prophets is the foundation of Christian faith, and the elect precious corner-stone, disallowed by the builders, has become their corner-stone as well, but a stumbling-stone and rock of offence, so that from unbelief they stumbled at the Word on which their whole building rests. Moses, the greatest prophet and the national law-giver, is but the smallest and most transient shadow of his office, which he himself confessed to be the mere prototype of another prophet, whose raising up he promised to his brothers and their successors, with the express command to obey him. The golden calf of Egyptian tradition and Rabbinic human ordinances, introduced by Aaron and the chiefs of the synagogue in the semblance of divine reason (for the sake of the Eternal!), was complete destruction of the law, in accordance with their own prophecy. Through this last abomination of desolation Moses became the Pope of the desecrated nation, the corpse of his putrefied law-giving became the relic of superstition, houses of prayer became dens of thieves, Bethel became Bethaven, and the city of the bridegroom of blood, in spite of heathen and anti-Christian Rome, became a Babylonian harlot and school of the dominant accuser, slanderer, liar and murderer from the beginning.

Christianity, therefore, does not believe in philosophical tenets, which are nothing but alphabetical scribaceousness of human speculation, subject to the fickle changes of the moon and of fashion; it does not believe in images and the worship of images, or of animals and heroes; it does not believe in symbolic elements and slogans, or a few black strokes written by the invisible hand of Chance on the white wall[1]; it does not believe in pythagorean-platonic numbers, or in any fugitive shadows of impermanent and unlasting actions and ceremonies, to which are ascribed a mysterious power and inexplicable magic, or in any laws which are to be obeyed even without believing in them (as the theorist says somewhere, in spite of his epicurean-stoic word-splitting about faith and knowledge). No: Christianity knows no other fetters of faith save the firm prophetic word in the most ancient documents of the human race and in the holy scriptures of genuine Judaism, without Samaritan separation and apocryphal Mishnah.

[1] " In the temple of Providence " everything is empty: " only a few black strokes on the white wall (the words God, All-wise, Almighty, All-good, reward the good) written perhaps by Chance. But the whole congregation gazes at these strokes with reverence, folds its hands before them, and worships them"; Mendelssohn, *Jerusalem*, Berlin, 1783, 335-6.

It was that deposit which made the Jews a people for his possession, instructed in divinity, anointed, and called and chosen before all peoples of the earth for the salvation of mankind . . .

But since the gods of the earth have made themselves the supreme philosophers, Jupiter (once *summus philosophus*) has had to creep into the cuckoo form of a pedagogue; and though Herr Mendelssohn seems to some extent to chide his departed friend[1] for picking up from who knows what historian the idea of the divine education of the human race, yet he himself has not only changed the idea of religion and the church into that of a public educational establishment, but in this schoolmasterly concern he has also repeated parrot-like so much trivial stuff about the leading-strings of language and Scripture and their natural parallelism with the religious power of masoretic literalism and scholastic verbiage, that a devout reader can scarcely help yawning at least at one point of his speculative slumber. For on Herr Mendelssohn's view it is a completely ungrounded article of faith to regard " the alphabetical language as mere signs of sounds." In accordance with his grounds of reason, *invita Minerva experientiæ*, the way from writing to the thing is no less than necessarily by and through language. Yet he asserts with almost incredible and unpardonable conviction that writing is " the direct description of the thing." What a pity that only philosophers who are born deaf can claim this privilege ! . . .

Unbelief in the most real historical sense of the word is therefore the only sin against the spirit of true religion, whose heart is in heaven and whose heaven is in the heart. The mystery of Christian devotion does not consist of services, sacrifices and vows, which God demands of men, but rather of promises, fulfilments and sacrifices which God has made and achieved for the benefit of men; not of the finest and greatest commandment

---

[1] Lessing, died 1781.

which he has imposed, but of the supreme good which he has given; not of law-giving and moral teaching which have to do merely with human dispositions and human actions, but of the performance of divine decrees by means of divine acts, works and measures for the salvation of the whole world. Dogmatics and Church law belong solely to the public institutions of education and administration, and as such are subject to the arbitrary will of the authorities, being sometimes a rough and sometimes a fine outward discipline, according to the elements and degrees of the dominant æsthetic. These visible, public and common institutions are neither religion nor wisdom from above, but are earthly, human and devilish, according to the influence of foreign cardinals or ciceroni, poetic confessors or prosaic pot-bellied priests, and the changing system of statistical equipoise and preponderance, or of armed tolerance and neutrality—Churches and schools, like miscarried creatures of the state and of reason, have often sold themselves as infamously to the state and reason as betrayed them. Philosophy and politics have needed the sword of superstition and the shield of unbelief for all their common deceits and violence, and by their love as well as their hate have mishandled dogmatics more severely than Amnon did the sister of his brother Absalom.

In the infinite mis-relation of man to God " public institutions concerned with the relation of man to God " are sheer unrhymed sentences in dry words which infect the inner sap the more a speculative creature sucks in of it. First of all, in order to abolish the infinite mis-relation, before one can speak of relations which are to serve as the basis of connection for public institutions, man must either participate in a divine nature, or the godhead must assume flesh and blood. The Jews with their divine law-giving, and the naturalists with their divine reason have seized a protective palladium for levelling down this mis-relation. Consequently, no other mediating concept is left for the Christians and the

Nicodemuses but to believe with all their heart and soul and mind that God so loved the world ... This faith is the victory which has overcome the world. ...

Even a David Hume judaises and prophesies, like Saul the son of Kish. When Philo, the Pharisee, finally confesses to the hypocrite Cleanthes an access of astonishment and melancholy from the greatness and obscurity of the unknown object, and " his contempt of human reason, that it can give no solution more satisfactory with regard to so extraordinary and magnificent a question " as that of his own existence, then the whole piety of natural religion is lost in the Jewish anachronism of a " longing desire and expectation that Heaven would be pleased to dissipate, at least alleviate, this profound ignorance " by means of some other gospel than that of the cross, and some Paraclete (" adventitious instructor ") who is to come ...

Faith and doubt affect man's ability to know, as fear and hope affect his appetitive instinct. Truth and untruth are instruments of the understanding: (true or untrue) ideas of good and evil are instruments of the will. All our knowledge is in part, and all human grounds of reason consist either of faith in truth and doubt of untruth, or of faith in untruth and doubt of truth. " This (partly negative, partly positive) faith is prior to all systems. It produced them in order to justify itself," says the honourable friend[1] of Herr Moses Mendelssohn. But if the understanding believes in lies and enjoys it, doubts truths and despises them with disgust as bad food, then the light in us is darkness and the salt in us has lost its savour—religion is pure church parade, philosophy is an empty word-display, superannuated and meaningless opinions, out-of-date rights without power. Scepticism about

[1] Christian Garve, 1742-98, translator of Adam Ferguson's *Institutes of Moral Philosophy*, Leipzig, 1772.

the truth and credulity of self-deceit are thus as inseparable symptoms as cold and heat in a fever. The man who thinks that he is farthest from this sickness of the soul and most earnestly desires to cure it in all his fellow-men, himself confesses that he has tried so many times to exercise this cure on himself and on others that he has realised how difficult it is, and how small the success. Woe to the wretched man who finds anything to take exception to in these modest and chastened words!

What is truth? A wind that blows where it lists, whose sound one hears, but does not know whence it comes and whither it goes—a spirit whom the world cannot receive, because it neither sees him nor knows him.

Gentle reader, what does the peace which the world gives concern you and me? We know perfectly that the day of the Lord will come as a thief in the night. If they say, Peace, there is no danger! then disaster will overtake them quickly. And he, the God of peace, who is higher than all understanding, sanctify us wholly, that our whole spirit and soul and body be preserved blameless at the coming . . .

He who testifies to these things says, Surely I am coming soon. Amen.

A FLYING LETTER TO NOBODY
WHOM EVERYBODY KNOWS

1786

In its second version this work is a reply to a hostile review of *Golgotha and Scheblimini*, and is a kind of justification of Hamann's whole authorship, in contrast to the kind of writing and thinking characterised by Mendelssohn's *Jerusalem*. I give here, however, a few paragraphs from the first version, in which Hamann reflects upon the categories which determine his whole writing, especially the meaning of "presence." Kierkegaard's concern with the "moment," and the phenomenologist's concern with the unfolding of man's being, out of himself, in the present, are both foreshadowed here. Dr. Wilhelm Koepp, in a recent article (see Bibliography), has carefully examined the significance of the changes Hamann made, and concludes that Hamann here renounces what was later to be known as " existentialism." Certainly this is true, so far as existentialism is considered to be a way of human life which produces out of itself a positive content. But it is still possible to see a more potent existentialism, more potent even, because more aware of the *communicatio idiomatum*, than Kierkegaard's, in Hamann's whole conception. That is, Hamann perceived, in the givenness of human existence, at the same time a revelation of God's existence. The Christian existentialist sees his given life at the same time as a sign of this revelation; and sees his task to be a witness, a signpost. Nor need we excise the first version of *The Flying Letter* from Hamann's authorship. If he had had time, both the first and the second versions would have become separate writings.

A FLYING LETTER

THE SPIRIT of observation and the spirit of prophecy are the wings of human genius. Everything that is present belongs to the province of the former; everything that is absent, in the past and the future, to the province of the latter. Philosophical genius expresses its power by striving, by means of abstraction, to make the present absent, unclothing real objects and making them naked concepts and merely thinkable attributes, pure appearances and phenomena. Poetic genius expresses its power by transfiguring, by means of fiction, the visions of the absent past and future into present representations. Criticism and politics resist usurpation by both powers, and try to preserve a balance by means of the same positive forces and means of observation and prophecy.

The present is an indivisible, simple point, in which the spirit of observation is concentrated, and from which it has its effect upon the whole sphere of the common power of knowing. The absent has a twofold dimension, being divisible into past and future, corresponding to the similarly ambiguous spirit of prophecy, to which the instinct which was recently (in the grey twilight of the seventh *Morgenstunde*[1]) divided into our capacity of approval

> laudator temporis acti
> se puero—

[1] *Morgenstunden, oder Vorlesungen über das Dasein Gottes* (" On the Existence of God "), by Moses Mendelssohn, Berlin, 1785.

and our capacity for desire—*avidusque futuri*—seems to be related.

Since therefore the sum of the present is infinitely small over against the manifold aggregate of the absent, and the spirit of prophecy is infinitely superior to the simple spirit of observation, our power of cognition depends on the many-headed modifications of the inmost, obscurest and deepest instincts of approval and desire to which it must be subject. . . .

. . . Despite my arbitrary division of the intellectual universe into presence and absence, I admit that these predicates are no more than subjective conditions from which no conclusion can be drawn about any twofoldness of the objects themselves, but only about a relation of the different views of one and the same thing to the corresponding measure of the inward man, of his negative, transient and finite power, which is not capable of any omnipresence, since this is the exclusive property of positive immeasurability.

Similarly, the spirit of observation and the spirit of prophecy are expressions of a single positive power, which cannot be divided in their nature, but only in thought and for use; and in fact presuppose one another, are related to and mutually affect one another. Hence when I compared the present to an indivisible point, the twofoldness of its power and of its very close connection with the past as effect and with the future as cause is not in the least abolished. Presence and absence can as well be predicates of one and the same object as—[*here author's MS. breaks off.*]

This is at the same time another proof of the unbreakable bond between the spirit of observation and the spirit of prophecy. Certainly we know in part, and prophesy in part[1]; but united they are a threefold cord which cannot easily be broken. If one falls his comrade helps him up; and if they lie together they warm one another.[2] What would the most exact and careful knowledge of the present be without a divine renewal of the past, without an

[1] I Cor. 13. 9.   [2] Eccles. 4. 10-12.

inkling of the future, as Socrates had to thank his *daimon* for? What a labyrinth the present would be for the spirit of observation, without the spirit of prophecy and its clues from the past and the future! The spirit of prophecy rains its gifts even upon the rebellious,[1] that God the Lord may dwell there incognito, without their will or knowledge . . .

[1] Psalm 68. 18.

LETTERS AND
MISCELLANEOUS WRITINGS

Out of the rich collection of letters only a handful of extracts is given here: first from those to Kant, together with a few interesting references to Kant culled from other letters; then a few passages about language, supplementing those given in the Introduction, and including the opening paragraphs of *The Knight of Rosenkreuz's Last Will about the divine and human Origin of Language*; and a selection from the letters to F. H. Jacobi dating from 1783 to 1787. The section concludes with a brief but pregnant passage from *Zweifel und Einfälle (Doubts and Ideas)*, 1776.

LETTERS AND
MISCELLANEOUS WRITINGS

LETTERS TO KANT

. . . If you are Socrates and your friend wishes to be Alcibiades, then for your instruction you need the voice of a *genius*. And this role is due to me, without my incurring the suspicion of pride—an actor lays aside his royal mask, his stilted gait and speech, as soon as he leaves the theatre—so allow me to be called *genius* and to speak with you out of a cloud as long as I am writing this letter. But if I am to speak as a *genius* I beg for the patience and attentiveness with which an exalted, fair, witty and learned public lately heard the farewell speech of a mortal concerning the fragments of an old urn on which one laboriously deciphered the letters BIBLIOTEK . . .

I write in epic style, because you cannot yet read lyric language. An epic author is a historian of rare creatures and their still rarer course of life; the lyric author is the historian of the human heart. Self-knowledge is the hardest and highest, the lightest and most loathsome natural history, philosophy and poetry. It is pleasant and profitable to translate a page of Pope—into the fibres of the brain and the heart—but vanity and a curse to look through a part of the *Encyclopédie* . . .

If I had to justify myself, then I should have to prove
    1. that my friend [Berens] has a false knowledge of himself,
    2. judges every one of his neighbours just as falsely,
    3. had and still has a false knowledge of me,

4. judges wrongly and one-sidedly the affair between us, as
   a whole and in its context,

5. has no conception or sensitiveness concerning what he
   and I have hitherto done and still do . . .

What your friend does not believe concerns me as little as it concerns him what I believe. In this we are quite separate, and we can talk only of business . . .

Abraham is our father—do we work according to Peter's model? . . . Truths can cause more harm than errors if we make a senseless use of the former, and know how to modify the latter by routine or chance. As many an orthodox person can go to hell, in spite of the truth, and many a heretic goes to heaven, despite the ban of the dominant church or of the public.

How far man can be effective in the order of the world, is a task for you; but a task which one cannot dare to undertake, until one understands how our soul is effective in the system of its small world. Whether *harmonia praestabilita* (pre-established harmony) is not at least a happier sign of this miracle than *influxus physicus* (natural influence) as an expression of this idea, I leave you to decide . . .

These reflections are nothing but apples which I throw as Galatea did to tease her lover. I am as little concerned with truth as your friend is; like Socrates I believe everything that the other believes—and I aim only at disturbing others in their belief. The wise man had to do this because he was surrounded by sophists and priests whose sound reason and good works existed only in their imagination. There are people who imagine that they are healthy and honourable, just as there are *malades imaginaires* . . .

He who believes more in another's reason than in his own ceases to be a man, and takes first place among the *servum pecus* of imitators. Even the greatest human genius is not good enough for us to imitate . . .

What are the archives of all kings and all centuries, if some lines of this mighty fragment, some dust in a sunbeam of this chaos, are able to give us knowledge and power? How happy is the man who can daily visit the archives of him who can lead the hearts of all kings like streams, whose pleasure it is to regard his wonderful economy and the laws of his kingdom. A pragmatic writer says of this, " The statutes of the Lord are more precious than gold, than much fine gold, sweeter than honey and the dripping honeycomb." " The law of thy mouth is better unto me than thousands of gold and silver." " I have more understanding than all my teachers, for thy testimonies are my meditation. I understand more than the ancients, because I keep —thou through thy commandments hast made me wiser than mine enemies; for they are ever with me."

What do you think of this system? I want to make my neighbours happy. A rich merchant is happy. For you to be rich needs insight and moral virtues.

In my mimic style there rules a stricter logic and a closer bond than in the ideas of lively brains. Their ideas are like the playing colours of shot silk, says Pope.

One moment I am a leviathan, the monarch or the prime minister of the ocean, from whose breathing come the ebb and flow of the tides. The next moment I regard myself as a whale whom God has created, as the greatest poet has said, to play in the sea.

I must almost laugh over the choice of a philosopher to bring about a change of mind in me. I look upon the best demonstration as a sensible girl looks upon a love-letter, and I look upon an explanation in the style of Baumgarten as a witty *fleurette*.

. . . Lies are the native language of our reason and wit.

One must not believe what one sees, let alone what one hears. When two men are in different positions, they must never dispute about their sense-impressions. A watcher in an observatory has much to tell to one who is in the third story. The latter must not be so stupid as to say that the watcher's eyes are defective. " Come down, and you will be convinced that you have seen nothing." A man in a deep ditch where there is no water can see the stars at noon. The man on the surface does not deny the stars, but he can only see the lord of the day. Because the moon is nearer the earth than the sun, you tell your moon stories about the glory of God. It is God's glory to conceal a thing, but it is the glory of kings to investigate a thing.

As one knows a tree by its fruits, so I know that I am a prophet from the destiny which I share with all witnesses, to be slandered, persecuted, and despised.

... The Attic philosopher, Hume, needs faith when he eats an egg or drinks a glass of water. He says that Moses, the law of reason, to which the philosopher appeals, condemns him. Reason is not given to you in order that you may become wise, but that you may know your folly and ignorance; as the Mosaic law was not given to the Jews to make them righteous, but to make their sins more sinful to them. If he needs faith for eating and drinking, why does he deny his own principle when he is giving his judgment about higher things than eating and drinking?

To explain something by custom—custom is a composite thing, consisting of monads. Custom is called second nature and its phenomena are just as enigmatic as nature which it imitates.

If only Hume were honest and consistent—yet despite all his errors he is like Saul among the prophets. I will transcribe a passage which will prove to you that one can preach the truth in jest and without knowing or desiring to do so, even if one were the greatest doubter and like the serpent doubted what God said. Here it is: " The Christian religion not only was at first attended with miracles, but even at this day cannot be believed by any reasonable person without one. Mere reason is insufficient to convince us of its veracity. And whoever is moved by Faith to assent to it, is conscious of a continued miracle in his own person, which subverts all the principles of his understanding, and gives him a determination to believe what is most contrary to custom and experience."

Tell your friend that it becomes him least of all to laugh at the spectacles of my æsthetic imagination, because I use them to arm the weak eyes of my reason.

. . . But a philosopher looks upon poets, lovers and projectors as a man looks upon a monkey, with pleasure and pity.

As soon as men understand one another they can work together. He who confused the languages—and as a friend of man punished the schemes of pride from love and politic reasons, for the good of man—joined them together again on the day when men with tongues of fire were slandered as being drunk with sweet wine. Truth did not want highwaymen to come too near her. She wore garment upon garment, till one doubted whether one would find her body at all. How terrified they were when they had their will, and they saw before them the terrible spectre, the truth!   *27 July*, 1759

From *A supplement of two love-letters to a Teacher of world wisdom* [Kant] *who wanted to write a physics book for children*, 1759

. . . The chief law of method for children consists in lowering oneself to their weakness; becoming their servant if one wishes to be their master; following them if one wishes to rule them; learning their language and soul if we want to move them to imitate our own. But this practical principle can neither be understood nor carried out unless, as one says in popular speech, one adores them, and loves them without properly knowing why . . .

These reflections are intended to move you to think of no other plan for your physics book than that which is already in the constitution of every child who is not a heathen or a Turk, and who is, so to speak, awaiting the culture of your instruction.

The best plan you could put in its place would have human defects, perhaps greater than the rejected corner-stone of Mosaic history or story. Since this contains in itself the origin of all things, a historical plan for a science is always better than a logical one, however artistic it may be. Nature in the six days of its birth is therefore the best scheme for a child, who believes this legend of its nurse until it can count and draw and prove; and thereafter does not do wrong to believe the numbers and figures and inferences as it once believed its nurse.

I am surprised that the wise Architect of the world thought of giving us an account of his labours at the great work of creation, since no clever man easily takes the trouble to enlighten fools and children about the mechanism of his actions. Only love towards us sucklings of creation could have moved him to this weakness.

How would a great mind set about enlightening a child that still went to school, or a simple maidservant, about his systems and projects? That it has been possible for God to make us grasp the slightest thing about the origin of things, is incomprehensible; and the actual revelation of it is as fine an argument for his wisdom as its apparent impossibility is a proof of our imbecility . . .

. . . the day before yesterday I received the first thirty sheets of the *Critique of Pure Reason*. Was abstemious not to look at them the same day, in order to do my stint of Voltaire. Yesterday I stayed the whole day at home, and after preparing myself with an ounce of Glauber's salt I swallowed the whole thirty sheets in one go (I lost the thread in the chapter on the Interest of Reason)—and I should think that the book will as little lack readers as Klopstock's *German Republic* lacked subscribers. I skipped a few sheets, because thesis and antithesis ran on opposite pages, and it was too troublesome to follow the double thread in a proof copy. It also seems to me to be clean of misprints; I have noticed about a dozen. The proof of the externals is very much in accordance with the author's wish. On a rough estimate I should suppose that the whole book will run more than twice through the alphabet. By human suppositions it will rouse interest and lead to new investigations, revisions, etc. But fundamentally very few readers will be fit for the scholastic content. As the book goes on the interest grows, and there are delightful and blossoming resting-places, after one has waded for a long time in the sand. In general, the work is rich in prospects—and in leaven for new fermentations both in and outside the faculty. Yet because the fate of no book can be reliably prophesied, I at least wish the briskest sale for it, I want to miss none of the inevitable criticisms of the learned heralds, and I thank you for the anticipated pleasure, with longing expectation of the end, and of the whole work, from sheet Hh to the Foreword.

To I. F. Hartknoch, 8 *April*, 1781

I am curious to hear your view of Kant's masterpiece. As one who heard his lectures you will be able to grasp much of it more quickly. He certainly deserves the title of a Prussian Hume. His whole transcendental philosophy seems to me to boil down to an ideal of entity. Without knowing it, his enthusiasm for the intellectual world beyond space and time is worse than Plato's. Here you really find language and technology the *deipara* of pure scholastic reason, and a new leap from Locke's *tabula rasa* to *formas et matrices innatas*. Both are wrong, and both are right; but how, and how far, is the point.

Hume is always my man, because he at least honours the principle of belief and has taken it up into his system. Our countryman keeps on chewing the cud of Hume's fury against causality, without taking this matter of belief into account. That does not seem to me to be honest. Hume's *Dialogues* end with the Jewish and Platonic hope of a prophet who is to come;

and Kant is more like a cabbalist who turns an *aion* into the godhead, in order to establish mathematical certainty, which Hume, excluding geometry, restricts more to arithmetic.

To Herder, 10 *May*, 1781

Now what do Messrs. the metaphysicians on the Spree say to the Prussian *Critique of Pure Reason*, which could just as fittingly have been called mysticism, on account of its ideal—which stops the mouth of all the speculative theology of the Spaldings and Steinbarts, etc., etc., and the Jesuit reflections of our Hephaestuses?

To J. F. Reichardt, 25 *August*, 1781

A week ago, in the morning, I received a bound copy of Kant. On 1 July I sketched a review *en gros*, but put it back in my files, because I did not want to give offence to the author, an old friend and I must almost say benefactor, since I had him to thank almost entirely for my first job. But if my translation of Hume should ever see the light of day, I will not mince matters, but say what I think.

To Herder, 5 *August*, 1781

My poor head is a broken pot compared with Kant's—earthenware against iron.

All chatter about reason is pure wind: language is its organ and criterion, as Young says. Tradition is the second element.

To Herder, 8 *December*, 1783

Kant has bound me by gratitude on account of my son, in order, like yourself, to avoid any disagreement. Setting aside the old Adam of his authorship, he is really a helpful and unselfish man, basically good and noble in his disposition, talented and worthy . . . Our knowledge is fragmentary; this great truth cannot be rightly felt by any dogmatician, if he is to play his part well; and scepticism itself, following an unavoidable circle of pure reason, becomes dogma.

To Herder, 8 *May*, 1785

Yesterday I visited our court preacher Schulz, who gave me the papers concerning a phenomenon which has caused quite a stir. It concerns a band of scoffers of religion, consisting of fifty students of theology. They call themselves Kantians . . .

To Herder, 18 August, 1785

Even if I were as eloquent as Demosthenes, I should not have to do more than thrice repeat a single phrase: Reason is language, *logos*. This is the bone I gnaw at, and shall gnaw myself to death over. Yet these depths are still obscure to me; I still await an apocalyptic angel with a key to this abyss.

To Herder, 6 *August*, 1784

No mathematical method is possible without mathematical figures; and that is a mathematical truth for me like the truth that every mass is equal to itself: you cannot get more out of words and explanations than you agree to put into them. The whole certainty of mathematics depends upon the nature of its language, the inevitability of all proofs depends upon the poetic licence of thinking metaphysical points, lines and surfaces which are physically impossible. What Demosthenes calls *actio*, Engel mimicry, and Batteux imitation of beautiful nature, is for me language, the organ and criterion of reason, as Young says. Here is to be found pure reason and its critique—and the eternal strife on the boundaries will last until languages end in prophecies and knowledge.

To Scheffner, 11 *February*, 1785

Your theme of language, tradition and experience is my

favourite idea, the egg I brood upon—my one and all—the idea
of mankind and its history, the goal and jewel which is pinned
to our common authorship and friendship.

To Herder, 9 *November,* 1785

If one presupposes God as the source of all effects, both large
and small, in heaven and on earth, then every counted hair of
our head is as divine as that behemoth, the " chief of the ways of
God." Then the spirit of the Mosaic laws is stretched to include
the most loathsome secretions of the human body. In consequence,
everything is divine, and the question about the origin of evil
ends in a play of words and chatter of the schools. But everything divine is also human; for man can neither work nor suffer
except according to the analogy of his nature, no matter how
simple or how artificial a machine this nature is. This *communicatio* of divine and human *idiomatum* is a basic law, and the
main key to all our knowledge and the whole visible economy.

Since the instruments of language at least are a present from
the *alma mater* Nature (with whom our strong spirits carry on a
more tasteless and blasphemous idol-worship than the heathen
and papist mob), and since, in accordance with the highest
philosophical probability, the Creator of these artificial instruments desired and had to establish the use of them as well, then
certainly the origin of human language is divine. But when a
higher being, or an angel, as with Balaam's ass, wants to work
through our tongues, then all such effects, as with the speaking
animals in Æsop's Fables, must be expressed in analogy with
human nature: and in this connection the origin of language
and still more its progress cannot be or appear anything but
human. Thus we find Protagoras speaking of man as *mensuram
omnium rerum.*

The Knight of Rosenkreuz's Last Will
(R IV, 21 = N III, 27)

LETTERS TO JACOBI

Reason to me is like God (the ideal of pure reason according to our Kant) for the ancient philosopher[1]: the longer I study the matter, the less I advance with this ideal of the godhead, or idol— " that is the nature of passion, that it cannot cling to the thing itself, but only to its image,"[2] and is it not the nature of reason to cling to the idea? . . . Become like children in order to be happy, is hardly the same as Have reason, have clear ideas! Law and prophets speak of passion with the whole heart and soul and powers—of love. While we are aiming at clear ideas the food gets cold and tasteless. You know that I think of reason as St. Paul does of the whole law and its righteousness—that I expect of it nothing but the recognition of error, and do not regard it as a way to truth and life . . .

But I have quite given up this investigation, on account of its difficulty, and cling now to the visible element, the organ or criterion[3]—I mean language. Without the word—no reason, no world. Here is the source of creation and government! What is sought in oriental cisterns lies in the *sensu communi* of the usages of language, and this key transforms our best wiseacres into senseless mystics, and the simplest Galileans and fishermen into the profoundest students and heralds of a wisdom which is not of earth, or of man, or of the devil, but a secret and hidden wisdom of God, which God ordained before the ages for our glory—which none of the rulers of this world can understand— I Cor. 2—and this philosophy leaves no proper man, who has been driven by fear into desert places and wilderness, without help and comfort.

2 November, 1783

[1] Simonides; cf. Cicero, *de natura deorum* I, 22.
[2] From the writing: *Etwas, das Lessing gesagt hat.*
[3] Cf. Young, *Night Thoughts*: Speech thought's canal, speech thought's criterion too.

... All metaphysical studies have recently, on account of the *Critique of Pure Reason*, become almost as loathsome to me as they were formerly on account of Wolff's Latin *Ontology*.

For me the question is not so much What is reason? as What is language? It is here I suspect the source of all paralogisms and antinomies can be found which are ascribed to reason: it comes from words being held to be ideas, and ideas to be things themselves. In words and ideas no existence is possible. Existence is attached solely to things. No enjoyment arises from brooding, and all things—including the *ens entium*—are there for enjoyment and not for speculation. The tree of knowledge has deprived us of the tree of life—and ought not the tree of life to be dearer to us than the tree of knowledge—do we always want to follow the example of the old Adam rather than see ourselves in his reflection, do we not want to become children, and like the new Adam share in flesh and blood, and take the cross upon ourselves? All the terminology of metaphysics comes in the end to this historical fact, and *sensus* is the principle of all *intellectus* ...

... He created man in his image, in the image of God he created him—we are his offspring. The *differentia specifica* lies simply in that we are still being made, and our life is still hidden with Christ in God. Our reason must wait and hope—and be servant, not law-giver, to nature ...

Experience and revelation are one, and indispensable wings or crutches of our reason, if it is not to be lame, and crawl. Sense and history are the foundation and ground—however deceitful the former may be, however simple the latter, I prefer them to all castles in the air. Δός μοι ποῦ στῶ—only no refined, abstract and empty words—these I avoid like deep still waters and slippery ice.

... A child that knows nothing is not for that reason a fool or a beast, but is still a man *in spe*. I know enough, if I exercise myself in sensibility (*Empfinden*)—and the less you know the more you can do. Knowledge puffs up, but love builds up. All is vanity—nothing new under the sun—is the end of all metaphysics and wisdom of the world, of which all that is left to us is the desire, the hope, and the foretaste of a new heaven and a new earth—in lovely and gracious but also passing and fugitive moments, like the ecstasies of love.

14 November, 1784

Being is certainly the one and all of everything. But the τὸ ὄν of ancient metaphysics has unfortunately been transformed into an ideal of pure reason, whose being and non-being cannot be determined by it. Original being is truth, communicated being is grace. Non-being is a lack, perhaps also an appearance of both, whose manifold nothingness has led to a loss of unity and centre. Thus it was with Spinoza and perhaps Lessing.

Metaphysics has its language of the schools and of the court. I suspect both, and I am not in a position either to understand them or to make use of them. Hence I am inclined to think that our whole philosophy consists more of language than of reason, and the misunderstandings of countless words, the posing as real of the most arbitrary abstractions, the antitheses of pseudo-gnosis,[1] and even the commonest figures of speech of the *sensus communis*, have produced a whole world of questions which have as little reason to be raised as to be answered. We are still needing a grammar of reason, as of writing and its common elements, which intermingle like the strings on the psaltery and yet sound together.

God, nature and reason are related as closely to one another as the light, the eye and everything the light reveals to the eye, or as the centre, the radius and the periphery of a circle, or as

---

[1] Cf. I Tim. 6. 20: "the contradictions of what is falsely called knowledge."

author, book and reader. Where is the riddle of the book? In its language or in its content? In the author's plan or the commentator's spirit? ——But my *crassa Minerva* would rather calve than go on ploughing.[1]

1 December, 1784

A world without God is a man without a head—without a heart, or entrails, or generative organs.

I have repeated *ad nauseam* that the philosophers are just like the Jews: neither of them knows what reason or the law is, or what they are given for—for the recognition of sin and of ignorance, not of grace and truth, which must be historically revealed, and cannot be attained by thinking, or by inheritance, or by working for it.

16 January, 1785

In Spinoza's first formula, *causa sui*, lies the whole error of logomachy. A relative term can by its nature not be thought absolutely without its correlative. Therefore (*effectus*) *causa sui* is at the same time (*causa*) *effectus sui*. A father who is his own son, and a son who is his own father. Is there such an example in the whole of nature? Spinozism is therefore a view which contradicts nature, assuming as it does only one single existing thing, which is at the same time cause and effect, and can be infinitely thought and felt. Finite things are modifications of the infinitely thought and infinitely felt. One can as little identify what is thought and what is felt as one can identify cause and effect in one subject. Being is the cause and existence the effect! So idea and thing are one and the same? The word, a sign of the idea, and appearance, a sign of the thing, are one and the same? And there is no distinction, either in nature or in reason? Yet they are

---

[1] Cf. Judges 14. 18: " if ye had not ploughed with my heifer, ye had not found out my riddle "; and Horace, *Sat.* II, 2, 3.

distinct all the same—for reason gives you *genus*, and nature a *differentiam specificam*.

16 January, 1785

Here below we do not hear of any transformation or transfiguration into the divine nature, but of the old word re-birth. We are to become children in order to enter the kingdom of heaven, and this is not seen by any mortal eye, but happens without being seen.

22 January, 1785

Not *cogito, ergo sum*, but the other way round, or even more Hebraic, *est, ergo cogito*, and with the inversion of such a simple principle the whole system perhaps receives a different language and direction.

2 June, 1785

Do not forget the noble *sum* on account of the *cogito*. God created—there is no other proof of his existence than this.

15 January, 1786

In the kitchen, too, the gods are to be found, and what Descartes says about his *cogito* is brought home to me by the activity of my stomach.

G 476

Is there no other knowledge but *a priori*, and must one deduce the *sum* from the *cogito* alone?

28 December, 1785

I am quite at one with Herder that all our reason and philosophy amount to tradition. . . . For me it is not a matter of physics or theology, but language, the mother of reason and revelation, their alpha and omega. It is the two-edged sword for all truths and lies. So do not laugh if I have to attack the matter from this side. It is my old tune, but all things are made by it. Γνῶθι σεαυτόν.

28 *October*, 1785

Kant confessed to me that he had never studied Spinoza properly, and being wrapped up in his own system he has neither the desire nor the time to have anything to do with others.

3 *December*, 1785

For if it is fools who say in their heart, There is no God, those who try to prove his existence seem to me to be even more foolish. If that is what reason and philosophy are, then it is scarcely a sin to blaspheme it.

18 *February*, 1786

Resignation of every appearance of being for the sake of true being is how I translate your principle. Being does not permit itself to be resigned, it is not our property, whereas the appearance of being is all the more the property of art and politics. Inner composure = being. With appearance everything is changeable, shadow and unrest. Am I right, do you not mean this? Being cannot be thought in appearance, but alongside and with appearance, as every shadow is present not in light or in the body, but with the light and alongside the body.

15 *March*, 1786

Self-knowledge is and remains the secret of genuine authorship. It is the deep well of truth, which lies in the heart, in the spirit, from thence rises up to the heights, and flows out like a happy stream, through lips and pen, doing good without noise or flooding.

6 *April*, 1786

Do not depend on our Critic [Kant]—nor do you need to. Like his System, he is not a rock, but sand, in which one soon tires to walk. Let truth go its own straight way, and leave to each his freedom. In this way you travel safest and best. I am just as concerned as you can be that he comes out with his work ... Every attachment to a system is a leaven for the pure, sheer truth, and it does not agree with the milk-food of truth. We must be weaned from system; and for babes no strong wine can serve.

Kant's neutrality should therefore not upset you. All my obligations to him, and the fact that he lets Michael go to all his lectures, must not keep me from writing what I think. Nor do I fear to bear any envy or jealousy at his fame. I have had some hard tussles with him, and at times I have clearly been in the wrong. But he has always remained my friend, and you will not make him your enemy either, if you pay to truth that honour which you owe it and have promised. You must expect that every systematic thinker looks upon his system as a Roman Catholic does on his church, and the same principle that was Lessing's and Mendelssohn's seems also to be Kant's πρῶτον ψεῦδος—although he, I think, speaks more modestly and without hypocrisy of revelation, and seems to draw it within the scope of his interest.

9 *April*, 1786

Nature and reason are just as much correlative as opposite ... Scepticism and dogmatism can just as fittingly stand alongside one another as knowledge and ignorance, and doubt with both of them, the " contradictions of knowledge falsely so-called " with the plerophoria of judgment and will, the tares with the wheat, the changing hours and seasons with the regular course of nature.

23 *April*, 1787

Faith needs reason just as much as reason needs faith. Philosophy is composed of idealism and realism, as our nature is of body and soul. *Qui bene distinguit, optime definire potest*—and both are necessary for one's own instruction and for teaching others. It does not seem to me that realism and idealism can fittingly comprehend the content of reason, as is the case with the reason of the schools, and artistic and sectarian reason, but rather the other way round. The reason of the schools divides up into idealism and realism. The right and genuine reason knows nothing of this artificial distinction, which is not based in the material of the thing, and contradicts the unity which is, or at least should be, at the basis of all our ideas. . . .

What is the common way of word usage? Witnesses. Are relationships not things that have qualities? And is a real existence possible or thinkable without things, qualities and relationships?

Is sense-knowledge not more apodeictic than knowledge of reason? Does uncertain knowledge not need grounds of reason; why should certain knowledge need grounds?

Every philosophy consists of certain and uncertain knowledge: of idealism and realism: of sense and inference. Why should only uncertain knowledge be called faith? What are *not* grounds of reason? Is knowledge without grounds of reason possible, any more than *sensus* without *intellectus*? Synthetic beings are not capable of simple sense-experience (*Empfindung*), and still less of knowledge. Sense-experience in human nature can as little be separated from reason, as reason can from the senses. The affirmation of identical propositions simultaneously includes the denial of contradictory propositions. Identity and contradiction are of equal certainty, but often rest upon an optical or transcendental appearance, thoughts, shadows and word-plays. Language is the wax nose which you have stuck on, the cardboard which you hang before your Spinoza, and which swims on the top of your whole way of thinking like congealed fat. Sense-experience must be qualified by grounds of reason. Knowledge from faith is basically identical with the *nil in intellectu* . . .

27 *April*, 1787

Reason is for me an ideal whose existence I presuppose, but cannot prove by means of the ghost of the appearance of language and its words. My fellow-countryman [Kant] has used this talisman to raise the castle of his *Critique*, and by this talisman alone can the magic building be dissolved. It is not worth while wasting another word on the matter until we are agreed what everyone understands by reason and faith—not what Hume, you and I and he understand, but what the thing itself is, and if it is a thing at all. A general word is an empty skin which changes every moment and bursts with the tension and cannot hold air any more; is it worth while squabbling over savourless salt, or an empty hide? Reason is the source of all truth and all errors. It is the tree of the knowledge of good and evil. So both sides are right and both are wrong, those who worship it and those who blaspheme it. Faith is likewise the source of unbelief and of false belief or superstition. Out of the *same* mouth proceed blessing and cursing (James 3). The *adiutorium*, the help, language, is the seducer of our understanding and will always be so, until we turn back, turn home to the beginning and source and former state. *Petitio principii* is the antidote to the unauthentic use of things and their misunderstanding. Being, faith, reason are sheer relationships, which do not let themselves be treated as absolutes; they are not things, but pure concepts of the schools, signs for the understanding not for admiration, means of help to awaken and fix our attention, just as nature is a revelation not of itself but of a higher object, not of its vanity but of *His* glory, which is not visible save to eyes illumined and furnished with weapons, and can only be made visible under new conditions,

with new instruments and institutions, abstractions and constructions, which must just as much be given (not created out of the
blue), as the old elements.

29 April, 1787

Sense-experience and knowledge of reason both rest upon
relationships of things, of their qualities, with the tools of our
receptivity, as upon the relationships of our conceptions. It is
pure idealism to separate believing and sense-experiencing from
thinking. Community is the true principle of reason and
language, through which our sense-experiences and conceptions
are modified. This and that philosophy separate things which
cannot at all be parted: things without relationships, relationships without things. There are no absolute creations, any more
than there is absolute certainty . . .

Since everyone works at the analysis of other people's ideas,
and the synthesis of his own, no constancy is possible from both
sides, but a perpetual turning and an unavoidable change. . . .
Each of us wishes to transform philosophy as it has been till now,
hopes and works for this, and adds his mite. What in your
language is *being,* I should prefer to call the *Word.* It is the Word
which unites Moses and John, Christianity and Judaism, the
living and the dead—whose society was scattered and spoiled by
the tower of Babel, but who are of one mind through the dove-
like innocence of the Spirit which has no tyrannical fetters—
it is the Word which turns fellow-sinners into brothers of one
mind . . .

I still do not know what Hume or we really understand by
faith, and the more we talk or write about it the less would we
succeed in grasping this quicksilver. *Sat prata biberunt.* Faith is
not everybody's thing, nor is it communicable like merchandise;
but it is the kingdom of heaven and hell within us. To believe
there is a God and to believe there is no God, is an identical

contradiction. Between being and believing there is as little connection as between cause and effect, once the bond of nature has been cut. *Incredibile sed verum.*

30 April, 1787

Just as all kinds of unreason presuppose the existence of reason and its misuse, so must all religions bear a relation to the faith in a single, independent and living truth, which, like our existence, must be older than our reason, and hence cannot be known from the genesis of reason but by a direct revelation of the truth.[1] Since our reason draws the material of its concepts merely from the external relations of visible, sensuous, changing things, in order itself to shape them in accordance with the form of their inward nature, and to make use of them for its pleasure or service, so the ground of religion lies in our whole existence, and outside the sphere of our powers of cognition, which taken all together constitute the most casual and abstract mode of our existence. This is why all religions have a mythical and poetic vein, and a foolish and offensive form in the eyes of a heterogeneous, incompetent, ice-cold and cadaverous philosophy, which shamelessly ascribes to its educative art the higher destiny of our domination of the earth.

Among all the revelations of which the human soul is more often capable in dream than when the spirit is awake, no single one has such an inward, intuitive, fruitful relation to all the indeterminate capacities, inexhaustible desires, endless needs and passions of our nature, which seems to be just as dependent in its physical connection with heaven and earth as it is in its bodily bond with life and sex and society—there is no single plan save that revealed through Christ, the Head, and through the body of his church, which explains the mysteries of the supreme, sole majesty, most hidden and most desirous to communicate itself,

---

[1] " As being is to creation, so is truth to faith." Plato, *Timaeus*, 26.

in better analogy to the whole system of nature and human society and more fittingly to the most arbitrary laws of sound reason and the most necessary inferences of living experience. This mustard-seed of anthropomorphosis and apotheosis, which is hidden in the heart and mouth of every religion, appears here in the greatness of a tree of knowledge and of life in the midst of the garden—all philosophical contradictions and the whole historical riddle of our existence, the impenetrable night of its *terminus a quo* and its *terminus ad quem*, are resolved by the primal message of the Word become flesh. This witness is the spirit of prophecy and the reward of its promise, " a new name which no one knows save he who receives it."

Even though speculative thinkers lack the spirit to believe the basic teachings of Christianity concerning the glorification of humanity in the godhead and of the godhead in humanity by means of the fatherhood and the sonship, and to sing with our Lutheran church,

> The spring of life rises from him,
> Coming from high heaven out of his heart,

even though the Nicolaitans[1] are ashamed of the divine power and divine wisdom in the word of the cross, and are offended by it, it is supremely unreasonable wickedly to deny or to erase truths which in virtue of their determination are bound to be foolish and offensive to the natural man, and it is just as immoral and irresponsible to deprive others of these truths if the proclamation of them is part of the ethos of the citizen's profession, office and class.

Zweifel und Einfälle
(R IV, 328ff. = N III, 191ff.)

[1] C. F. Nicolai (1733-1811) was one of the leading figures of the *Aufklärung* in Berlin. His name had for H. a useful resemblance to the Nicolaitans of Revelation 2. 6 and 15, members of a gnostic sect.

... A man can receive nothing, except it be given him,

> " And if He gives it, he has it free,
> No one may inherit (transcendental Judaism)
> Nor win (philosophical Popery)
> Through works His grace
> Which has rescued us from death."

(The *ultimum visibile* and *summum bonum*, which makes us active and unhappy, or peaceful and happy.)

The tree of knowledge has robbed us of the fruit of life, and that tree is no means for the enjoyment of this goal and starting-point. The arts of the schools and the world intoxicate and puff up more than they can quench thirst.

To Thomas Wizenmann, 22 *July,* 1786

BIBLIOGRAPHY

EDITIONS

F. Roth, ed., *Hamanns Schriften*, seven volumes, Berlin, 1821-25 = R I, R II, etc.

J. Nadler, ed., *Werke*, six volumes, Vienna, 1949-57 = N I, N II, etc.

C. H. Gildemeister, ed., *J. G. Hamann's, des Magus im Norden, Leben und Schriften*, vol. 5, *Briefwechsel mit F. H. Jacobi*, Gotha, 1868 = G.

H. Weber, ed., *Neue Hamanniana*, Munich, 1905.

L. Schreiner and F. Blanke, ed., *Hamanns Hauptschriften erklärt*, vols. 1 and 7, Gütersloh, 1956.

ANTHOLOGIES

K. Widmaier, ed., *Schriften J. G. Hamanns*, Leipzig, 1921.

O. Mann, ed., *Hauptschriften Hamanns*, Leipzig, 1937.

P. Klossowski, *Les Méditations bibliques de Hamann*, Paris, 1948.

INDEPENDENT STUDIES
AND SIGNIFICANT REFERENCES

Hume, *Enquiry Concerning Human Understanding*, ed. Selby-Bigge, London, 1893.

Lessing, *Sämtliche Schriften*, ed. Lachmann and Muncker, Leipzig, 1897.

Kant, *Critique of Pure Reason*, ed. N. K. Smith, London, 1900.

Goethe, *Dichtung und Wahrheit*, book 12, 1812.

Hegel, Review of Roth's edition, 1828; see *Sämtliche Werke*, Jubiläumsausgabe, ed. Glockner, Stuttgart, 1930, XX, 240ff.

Amalie von Gallitzin, *Briefwechsel und Tagebücher*, n. F., Münster, 1876.

J. Disselhoff, *Wegweiser zu Johann Georg Hamann*, Kaiserswerth, 1871.

H. Weber, *Hamann und Kant*, Munich, 1904.

R. Unger, *Hamanns Sprachtheorie*, Munich, 1905.

H. Hettner, *Geschichte der deutschen Literatur im 18. Jahrhundert*, III, Leipzig, 1909.

R. Unger, *Hamann und die Aufklärung*, Jena, 1911.

J. Blum, *La vie et l'œuvre de J.-G. Hamann*, Paris, 1912.

F. Ebner, *Das Wort und die geistigen Realitäten*, Regensburg, 1921.

W. Lütgert, *Die Religion des deutschen Idealismus und ihr Ende*, II, Gütersloh, 1923.

F. Lieb, *Glaube und Offenbarung bei J. G. Hamann*, Munich, 1926.

E. Metzke, *J. G. Hamanns Stellung in der Philosophie des 18. Jahrhunderts* (in " Schriften der Königsberger Gelehrten Gesellschaft, Geisteswissenschaftliche Klasse "), 1934.

T. Schack, *Johann Georg Hamann*, Copenhagen, 1948.

E. Ermatinger, *Deutsche Dichter 1700-1900*, I, Bonn, 1948.

J. Wahl, *Études Kierkegaardiennes*, Paris, 1949.[2]

J. Nadler, *Johann Georg Hamann*, Vienna, 1949.

W. Lowrie, *Hamann—an Existentialist*, Princeton, 1950.

H. Schreiner, *Die Menschwerdung Gottes in der Theologie Johann Georg Hamanns*, Tübingen, 1950.[2]

R. Pascal, *The German Sturm and Drang*, London, 1951.

J. C. O'Flaherty, *Unity and Language*, Chapel Hill, 1952.

E. Hirsch, *Geschichte der neueren evangelischen Theologie*, IV, Gütersloh, 1952.

F. Blanke, *Hamann-Studien*, Zürich, 1956.

J. Macmurray, *The Self as Agent*, London, 1957.

M. Seils, *Theologische Aspekte zur gegenwärtigen Hamann-Deutung*, Berlin, 1957.

ARTICLES

R. Gregor Smith, " The Living and Speaking God," *Hibbert Journal*, 42, 1944.

P. Merlan, " Form and Content in Plato's Philosophy," *Journal of the History of Ideas*, VIII, 4, 1947.

P. Merlan, " Hamann et les Dialogues de Hume," *Revue de Métaphysique et de Morale*, 59, 1954.

P. Merlan, " Johann Georg Hamann," *Claremont Quarterly*, 3, 3/4, 1955.

W. Koepp, " J. G. Hamanns Absage an den Existentialismus," *Wissenschaftliche Zeitschrift der Univ. Rostock*, 1955/6, Gesellschafts- und Sprachwissenschaftliche Reihe, I.

E. A. Blackall, " Irony and Image in Hamann," *Publications of the English Goethe Society*, n.s. 26.

C. Hohoff, " Johann Georg Hamann—Magus im Norden," *Hochland*, 330, IV, 1957.

J. C. O'Flaherty, " Some Major Emphases of Hamann's Theology," *Harvard Theological Review*, LI, I, 1958.

Index

INDEX

Bold type indicates items in Selected Writings